COMMUNICATING IDEAS

11 Steps to Selling Innovation

Heath Row

10-10-10 PUBLISHING

D1409849

Table of Contents

Foreword by Tim Sanders

New York Times bestselling author of *Love Is the Killer App: How to Win Business and Influence Friends*

Heath Row knows how to communicate ideas effectively. I say that with years of experience knowing Heath through multiple phases of his career. Heck, he did so well communicating the idea of this book, I agreed to write my first foreword ever for a fellow author.

I first met Heath about 20 years ago over tapas in San Diego, the night before I spoke at *Fast Company* magazine's RealTime event to promote the launch of my first book. He created and then managed their Company of Friends community, and I was keen to spend time with him. In a short period of time, we bonded over music, business perspective, and what it takes to bring a meaningful idea to life.

Even then, Heath had a clear way of seeing the path of an idea from one's mind to the real world, and what it really took to move one along. At the time, he was locked into community-creating ideas, which at the turn of the 21st century was a nascent subject area.

In this, his first book, *Communicating Ideas*, Heath—now with more experience and career on his resume, including 13 years at Google—moves beyond team building at work and in local business communities and considers what might be the very root cause of community: communication.

This is not a book about marketing, though it will be useful to marketers. It is not a book about sales, though it will be useful to sales people. It is not a book for entrepreneurs, inventors, or startups, though they will find it useful, too. This is a book about the process of developing, enunciating, selling, and maintaining an innovation—which is fundamentally an *idea*.

What makes this read so valuable is how Heath maps your journey from the aha moment and your key ask, to how it's packaged, believed in, delivered, reinforced, and ultimately championed. Communicating a novel idea is all about moving others to action and making the world a better place.

Selling change is never easy. People like the way things are and are often held down by gravity when they try to embark on a transformative journey. Too often they frame the new as a threat instead of seeing it as an opportunity. That's why it's so hard to communicate a new idea in a way that resonates to the point of adoption. This book will give you rocket fuel to help propel others out of that space of safety into an adventure.

I recommend that you read this book over five reading sessions, taking in each section and then sleeping on it—or better yet, sharing some key concepts with a friend or co-worker. You'll get the most out of a book if you share its kernel, what I call the core concepts of the read. You can do that while it's still fresh in your mind or when you have a chance conversation with someone who has an idea that will require some communication savvy.

If you're new to communicating about new ideas, you'll find it a helpful guidebook that will walk you step by step toward cutting through the noise and clutter of competing ideas. And if you're a more experienced marketer, it'll take you back to basics and remind you to strip away the language of your trade to speak more plainly to win over your audience, regardless of your channel.

Whatever your situation, *Communicating Ideas* will help you become a more comfortable, competent—and confident—communicator.

That's an idea worth exploring!

—Tim Sanders
Prescott, Ariz.

Introduction
The Power of One Good Idea

"If you want to stand out from the crowd, give people a reason not to forget you."

—RICHARD BRANSON, BUSINESS PERSON

Over the course of my career—spanning more than three decades working in journalism, technology, business, marketing, research, education, and innovation—there has been one element common and consistent to the best work I've ever done, or encountered.

That common and consistent element is the *idea*.

Whether it's the article or story idea that inspires a writer, reporter, or editor—and in the end, a reader; the new technology, tool, or software that catalyzes the creative efforts of a new development team or business entity; the business idea that energizes the entrepreneur, startup team, or venture capitalist; the theme or topic that brings a gleam to the eye of a student; or the innovative concept or approach that captures the enthusiasm of the salesperson, marketer, or buyer; it is the *idea* that makes the world go 'round.

How we approach identifying and developing new ideas is important. Even more important, however, is how we let other people know about those ideas—how we *communicate* our ideas.

This volume captures some of what I've learned over my more than three decades as a journalist, writer, editor, project manager, marketer, researcher, educator, trainer, professional speaker, coach, and consultant. Regardless of whether I've been working for *Fast Company* magazine; building an online learning community with Seth Godin; teaching students at New York University or the University of Southern California; speaking to audiences at conferences around the world; managing research operations and projects or leading global marketing research training programs for Google; mentoring interns or younger colleagues just starting their careers; or working with a select group of private coaching and consulting clients, I have built my career on this topic: Communicating about ideas.

When my students ask me about big ideas that I've helped foster or further, I generally offer several just off the top of my head: Getting my son—now almost an adult himself—interested in Scouting before he was old enough to be a Cub Scout, proposing and planning a Route 66 summer vacation with my wife and son, launching the Company of Friends readers network for *Fast Company* magazine before social media even existed, and helping start the punk band the Anchormen.

Through those personal and professional experiences—communicating ideas and this book are not just for business people!—I learned a few lessons. For longer term goals or commitments—such as getting your child involved in a lifelong learning and leadership-development activity like Scouting—focus initially on short-term gains and immediate benefits. Focus on the fun and positive aspects, not the costs, commitments, or requirements for ongoing involvement over time. Securing initial interest in an idea—and only its upside—can help lessen the impact of any such costs once you're involved.

Even in situations where you might be tempted to, you can't just focus on benefiting yourself. You have to be sure you're meeting the needs of others involved. When proposing and planning a Route 66 summer vacation with my wife and son—from Santa Monica, Calif., to Albuquerque, N.M., the western half of the classic American road trip—I had to overcome concerns about vacation overscheduling that I'd subjected them to before. (Not everyone likes to walk around as much as I do. I like to walk around a *lot*.) I had to make sure that I was including locations and activities that everyone would find interesting. Sometimes you need to do something solely for the sake of others to deposit credits into that bank, too.

When I pitched the Company of Friends readers network to Alan Webber at *Fast Company* magazine, I focused on the signals I was seeing as an associate editor at the magazine. We'd positioned *Fast Company* as not just a magazine but a movement since its launch. Reader response was extremely energetic and enthusiastic; readers wanted to engage even more than they could at the time. Readers were similar psychographically despite diverse demographics—resonating with the magazine's themes of leadership and innovation. And readers were beginning to contact the magazine—responding to the weekly newsletter I edited at the time, *Fast Take*—asking if we could help connect them with other readers where they lived and worked. Using evidence—leading indicators—can help persuade stakeholders that there's a *there* there for your idea.

And finally, the Anchormen, the punk band that I sang in from 1997-2005, largely started as a joke. My housemate, Tom—I lived with three men named Tom at the time—and I talked about starting a band some day. Then we let another friend know about the half-baked plan, and then another. Soon we had four creative, energetic, talented people who enjoyed each other's company thinking that the band was perhaps less a joke and more an *idea*. And so the Anchormen were born. We ended up recording three CDs and playing multiple shows throughout Massachusetts, including live performances on WMBR-FM, participating in a multimedia arts collective called Handstand Command that developed its own following and fan base, sharing the stage (albeit briefly and perhaps unwillingly) with Evan Dando of the Lemonheads—earning us a press mention—and even performing on a stage area once graced by James Brown, the Godfather of Soul himself. Our records were reviewed relatively well by magazines such as *The Big Takeover*, *Hit List*, *Maximum Rocknroll*, and *Punk Planet*. Sometimes, creative friends are all you need to make an idea reality. And sometimes, even a seemingly silly or small idea is worth pursuing. Not every idea needs to be big or important.

Most of those ideas were primarily fun and enjoyable experiences, with little downside or hassle. But two of them brought their share of hardship and challenge—requiring hard work, focus, and drive. And one of them—the Company of Friends—was career defining early in my work experience. (Because of my work on the readers network, I was featured as one of the 40 Under 40 in *Folio:* magazine, as well as in *The New York Times Magazine*.) What started as a little database I maintained manually on my desktop grew into a network of about 45,000 people around the world, meeting face to face in about 165 cities in 35 countries. That seems small by current social media standards, but the network helped members find work, develop ideas, identify collaborators, mobilize resources, build companies, learn skills—even meet their future spouse. The network truly improved *Fast Company* readers' work lives, situations, and communities.

We now have the opportunity for me to help you make *your* ideas reality—to help you learn how to better communicate your ideas. I am writing this book to help you learn how to better prepare ideas for sharing with others; develop yourself to become an ideas-driven leader; more successfully persuade people about the merits of a given idea; and become more effective as a family or community member, friend, teammate, employee, sales person or marketer, innovator, speaker, or leader. In the end, I want to help you bring your best and brightest ideas to the world, for the benefit of as many people as possible.

This book documents my time- and trial-tested 11-step process to communicate ideas and sell—in the broadest most possible sense of the term—innovation. I've identified, implemented, and refined this process over my several decades as a professional. The steps are broken into five sections, highlighting the most important aspects of communication: your purpose, the packaging of your idea, the person communicating it, planning to do so, and the pitch itself.

Let's stick with that word for a moment: the "pitch." In communication—and in sales—too much attention is paid to the pitch itself. The pitch is the very end of the process. The pitch is the *release*, after which point you can't do anything more about it. You can't fix a pitch once you've thrown it.

As communicators, we can learn a lot from baseball. In baseball, players recognize that the pitch is the *end* of the process, and perhaps not really the most important part of the pitcher's job. Instead, it is the culmination of a long process of preparation that in fact determines the quality of the resulting pitch. You might consider the pitch the release, the wind up the pre-release, and the conditioning that takes place before and in between games as the pre-pre-release. All are important, and the pitch is nothing without the other two: conditioning and the wind up.

This book might seem different than other books focusing on concepts like the sales pitch, because I concentrate mostly on the conditioning and the wind up, as well as the release itself. But your release will be nothing without adequate focus on the other two parts of the preparation process.

Communicating Ideas is designed to walk you through that process step by step. Throughout the book, I've included select inspirational and provocative quotes from various leaders and innovators, as well as workbook prompts and elements under the heading "A Question for You." Because we don't dedicate a lot of space in the book for that workshopping and woodshedding as you read, you might find it worthwhile to read armed with a pencil or pen, as well as a notebook, journal, or other way to capture notes and thoughts as you proceed. Your notes, scribbles, contributions, and content created in response to those prompts will help you develop an ideas communications strategy and plan as you read *Communicating Ideas*. The book will be more useful and valuable to you if you read with a specific idea firmly in mind. And if you'd like to explore building that idea further with my support and assistance, just let me know. I'd love to help you.

I also include several "Communicating My Ideas" case studies, focusing on a number of ideas I've communicated over the years, and some of the lessons I learned as a result. One of those case studies further explores the Company of Friends, which I touched on above briefly to set the stage. Another one was a total failure. We can learn a lot from our failures, as we can our successes. Learning from both is productive.

An idea in one person's mind is just a glimmer, a spark. But once an idea is in the mind of more than one person, it can become a flame, a wildfire.

And together, we can change the world.

Section 1
Purpose

"If you don't have an emotional connection to why you are trying to accomplish your goals, the odds are you won't reach them or will quit trying."

—BRETT HOEBEL, PERSONAL TRAINER

Why do you do what you do? What keeps you up at night? And what keeps you going all day?

Some people might call such motivators your goals, dreams, desires, even values. For the purposes of this section, I call it your purpose. Whatever your purpose is, it is the reason you do what you do, through thick and through thin.

Sometimes your purpose will be personal: for your parents, a spouse, your children. Sometimes it might even be transactional: to put food on the table and to pay your bills. Sometimes it might be even more ambitious: to become your best possible self, and to bring the most light and love to your home, community, and relationships—however you define that.

At other times, your purpose will be professional. It will be tightly tied to and inspired by your job, your role or position in an organization, the goals of your manager and team, the requirements of your job, and your key performance indicators.

Usually, professional purpose is easier to identify. Personal purpose can be more challenging to determine. And combining your professional and personal purposes? Why, that's the dream for so many people.

Regardless, to communicate ideas clearly, you need a purpose. Why does the idea even matter? This section and the two steps it contains will help you identify, clarify, and document that purpose.

Step 1
Start with an Idea

"The mind that opens to a new idea never returns to its original size."

— ALBERT EINSTEIN, PHYSICIST

Ideas and Innovation

Before we get too far into the book, I want to do two things. First of all, I want to assert that this book is about *communicating ideas*, not coming up with or developing new ideas. We start off presuming that you already have an idea that you'd like to communicate—that you've already developed an idea. However, if you're interested in learning more about how to best develop new ideas, how to brainstorm, or how to create a new invention, I am willing and able to share my professional and personal experiences along those lines—and to help you identify other resources that can help.

For the purposes of this book, however, we will presume that you already have an idea.

Now, what to do with it?

If you're an individual contributor at a company, a member of a team within an organization, or a salesperson, you might have been *given* the idea or innovation that you are expected to successfully communicate. It might not be your own. If you are a small business owner or entrepreneur, you probably already have a commercial opportunity that you want to get across to potential clients and customers. If you are a team leader or executive, you already have a mission or vision that you want your team members and employees to support. And if you personally or professionally want to accomplish a goal or do something—in your life, with your family, with your friends, in or church, or otherwise—you already know what that is. You just need to learn how to most successfully communicate that idea or innovation, commercial (or non-commercial) opportunity, or goal.

I also want to be very clear about what an idea or an innovation is. According to the *Shorter Oxford English Dictionary*, sixth edition, an idea is "the plan or design according to which something is created or constructed," and "a conception of something to be done or achieved; an intention, a plan of action." In this book, we will focus more on ideas as suggested courses of action, aims, and purposes than we will on more abstract ideas, opinions, or beliefs. While ideas are important in and of themselves, what you *do* with an idea—what happens *next*—is even more important. We want the ideas we choose to communicate to help people make decisions, solve problems, accomplish a task, and otherwise do something. You could consider such ideas as Solutions-Oriented Ideas.

What, then, are innovations? Again, the *Shorter Oxford English Dictionary*, sixth edition, suggests that an innovation is "the introduction of a new thing; the alteration of something established," "the introduction of a new product on to the market," and "a new practice, method, etc." That brings us even closer to Solutions-Oriented Ideas. Additionally, innovation as a noun can be the end result of the verb innovate, or the practice or process by which an innovator—one who innovates—builds on, changes, or improves an existing method, practice, organization, product, or structure.

A Question for You

What idea or ideas do you have that you'd like to better communicate? (Just a brief description of two or three specific ideas is fine for now. We'll expand on this—and choose one to focus on—as the book progresses.)

_____

_____

_____

_____

_____

Are your ideas *ideas*, or innovations? Why do you say so?

_____

_____

_____

_____

Ideas Matter

Why do ideas matter, anyway? Ideas matter because they are the building blocks of new thoughts, practices, processes, products, and experiences in the world. Ideas can inspire energy, hope, joy, and other emotions that can help us take on and overcome new challenges. Ideas can also help us solve problems and make decisions. They can also just be fun. (Like the Anchormen, for example.)

As people, creators, and business people, we can occasionally be judged based on the quality, and sometimes quantity, of our ideas. If you work for a company or are visible as a professional within an industry—even just as a team member where you work—you can position yourself as a progressive, productive contributor in your team, company, and industry based on the quality and quantity of your ideas. Ideas even matter in other settings such as community groups and volunteer organizations, churches and spiritual communities, and groups of friends—even families.

If ideas matter, how we communicate ideas also matters. If we want our ideas to be well received by others, to inspire action and energy, and to otherwise come to life in our work and life with others, we have to be sure that our ideas are easy to comprehend, understand, and act on. People will judge our ideas in part based on how we communicate those ideas. The less confident or competent we seem, the less solid or strong our ideas will seem.

It is important for our energy and inspiration behind an idea to translate for—and resonate with—other people. "Ideas make the world, for they are the guide to future practice," Ash Amin and Michael O'Neill wrote in their book *Thinking About Almost Everything.* "Even the flimsiest ideas rooted in prejudice and ignorance make history and form public culture.... Ideas, when mobilised, become the templates of thought and practice."

Our world is built on and by ideas. The quality of those ideas matter. And our ability to communicate good ideas—worthwhile ideas—matters even more.

A Question for You

Why are your ideas important? Why do they matter? (We'll also develop this as the book progresses. For now, just write a brief description of your idea's—or ideas'—importance.)

_____

_____

_____

_____

Types of Innovation and Ideas

In the 2015 *Harvard Business Review* article "You Need an Innovation Strategy," Gary P. Pisano categorizes innovations based on whether they require new technology, new business models—or both. His four categories of innovations—Routine, Radical, Disruptive, and Architectural—offer a useful framework for identifying what kind of innovation you might be working with.

Similarly, in the 2017 *Harvard Business Review* article "The 4 Types of Innovation and the Problems They Solve," Greg Satell offers four slightly different kinds of innovation. Suggesting that innovations at their most basic are solutions to problems—and considering how well a given domain of knowledge, problem, or challenge is already defined—Satell proposes that innovations can be categorized as Basic Research, Breakthrough Innovation, Sustaining Innovation, and Disruptive Innovation. (All of which can be lightly mapped against Pisano's matrix.) "Most innovation [is sustaining innovation], because most of the time we are seeking to get better at what we're already doing," Satell wrote.

Can *ideas* also be categorized? The staff of the online ideas incubator Ideas-Shared contends that there are four general kinds of ideas: things, achievements (accomplishments or goals, perhaps), processes, and concepts. Arguably, concepts can also perhaps evolve into a thing, achievement, or process.

Another way to think about ideas, however, is the setting in which they're relevant. Some of you might be wanting to discuss an idea with your family; for example, where you'd like to go for summer vacation next year, or what movie you'd like everyone to watch on the next family movie night. (At the time of this writing, my family is currently working its way through the output of Studio Ghibli, a wonderful idea proposed by my son. We recently watched *The Secret World of Arietty*.) Others of you might want to persuade a church group, volunteer organization, or other community group to undertake an activity or project, such as a fundraiser or letter-writing campaign. A few of you might want to pitch your team at work on a new project or knowledge management software or system that you think would help make collaboration more efficient and effective. Perhaps you want to persuade your boss or manager to consider a new product or service idea. Maybe you work in sales and need to drum up business among new or already active accounts and clients. You might even be the founder of a startup who plans to meet with venture capital firms or business incubators and accelerators to raise funds and otherwise help expand your startup.

In my three decades working as a business and technology journalist, startup director, marketer, research operations manager, educator, and professional speaker, I've learned that how we communicate ideas—regardless of how they're categorized, or the setting in which we're involved—is consistent. What we are communicating might differ depending on the idea, but *how* we communicate it will only vary slightly depending on the type of idea or innovation, or our situation.

This book—*Communicating Ideas*—will be useful for communicators of all sorts regardless of the idea itself. You do not have to work in business or technology to implement the ideas contained herein.

A Question for You

What kind of idea are the ideas you're considering? What kind of innovation do your ideas involve?

What kind of situation or organization are you involved in?

Gauging Good Ideas

Even though I presume that you already have an idea in mind as you read this book, it might be helpful to spend a minute considering how you can gauge whether your idea is a good idea. Some innovation wags might joke that good ideas are like obscenity: "I know it when I see it." But there are qualities and characteristics you can look for and consider to determine whether an idea is good—or at least likely to be considered good by other people. (You might not be the best judge of whether an idea you developed or are otherwise invested in is a good idea. It's always important to validate that with others. We'll explore that later.)

Keith Harmeyer and Mitchell Rigie, innovation consultants and authors of the book *SmartStorming*, suggest that good ideas generally possess the following elements:

1. Different or Better—An idea must be somewhat different and offer some degree of improvement.
2. Delivers Value—The idea must do something better (faster, cheaper, easier, more elegantly, more powerfully, more effectively, more efficiently). That improvement must be something somebody actually wants.
3. Doable—For an idea to be good, it has to be possible.
4. Acceptable Cost-Benefit—If an idea costs more to implement than the value it delivers, it is impractical. The benefit must outweigh the cost.

Similarly, creativity consultant Richard Holman recommends several additional universal qualities of a good idea—especially through the lens of marketing creative and advertising:

1. Simplicity
2. Originality

3. Truth
4. Craft
5. Reward

Regardless of what elements or qualities you check your idea against, it's important that you seek the input of other people. They might be better judges of whether your idea is a good idea. As you'll learn later in this book, how others respond to your idea will help you learn how to better and more effectively communicate your idea in the future.

A Question for You

Why are your ideas good ideas? What elements or qualities of a good idea do your ideas possess?

_____

_____

_____

_____

_____

Who can you ask for input on the relative merit of your ideas?

_____

_____

_____

_____

_____

Picking a Winner

The above sets of characteristics can help you consider and determine whether an idea is a good idea. If you have multiple ideas, they might not entirely help you identify which single idea is the best idea. If you're choosing from among multiple ideas, the best idea might be the idea that most people like most, the idea that is most likely to be produced, the idea that costs the least to produce, the idea that people are willing to pay the most for—or some other combination of phrases including "most" and "best." Sometimes, but not always, the best idea is the idea that *you* like best.

The important thing is that you have one idea in mind as you read the rest of this book. As you continue to read—as we proceed through this 11-step process—you will apply the subsequent steps to your singular idea specifically.

If you like *all* of your ideas, don't worry about it. You can implement this process more than once for any idea you want to communicate, now and in the future.

A Question for You

As you read this book, based on the outcome of the above exercise, what is your best, favorite, or most promising current idea? What is the specific idea that you'll be thinking about as we continue to work through the 11 steps?

You have just completed Step 1, "Start with an Idea"—and identified your idea itself. In the next chapter, you'll take the next step: Now
that you have an idea, what do you want other people to *do* about it?

Step 2
Land on an Ask

"As long as people are clear on what they need to do and what's going on, you're very likely to succeed. When nobody is clear, then you're guaranteed to fail."

—BEN HOROWITZ, VENTURE CAPITALIST

What's in It for You? (Part One)

Before you can start thinking about how to best communicate an idea to someone else, it's important to understand why you want to communicate it to them—or communicate *with* them—in the first place. Taking time to do this, and doing so with some rigor, will help you better understand your potential audience—the people you're communicating with. It will also help you better understand just what you should be communicating about and even improve who you are—and how you are—as the person communicating with them.

If you don't have a vested interest in someone learning about your idea, a strong motivation for communicating it well, or a reason why you care, it will be extremely challenging for you to focus on communicating effectively. Sometimes that vested interest is obvious, particularly where the idea is given to you: You're a sales person, you work in marketing, or you need to persuade someone on the relative merits of an idea because of—on behalf of—your employer or parent organization. Sometimes, though, you might be passionate about an idea for another reason. Perhaps you'd like your Bible study group or spiritual study circle to focus on a specific text, topic, or theme collectively because it's of particular interest or relevance to you at this stage in your spiritual development. Maybe you'd like a neighborhood council to write letters about a community issue to local newspapers, or to write letters of support to political prisoners or community activists behind bars. Maybe you'd like to mobilize people to participate in a political protest or rally.

You might have an even stronger motivation to communicate an idea to potential business partners, customers, clients, or investors. For example, you might be the founder of a business or work as an independent consultant, coach, or business service provider. You might have even invented a new product you'd like to produce, distribute, or sell.

Helen Horyza, a career and job search professional, indicates that you can determine the motivation of you and your team—if you're working with others—by identifying your values. Ask everyone to list their top three values. That can be considered their motivation, and you can tie your organizational goals to those values. Doing so will increase investment in communicating the idea, and sometimes it can help identify who the best person to communicate the idea might be.

In any event, it's important for you to know why *you* are communicating a certain idea. What's in it for you? Why do you care?

A Question for You

Why do you care about this idea? Why are you the best person to communicate this idea?

What Do You Want?

After you've identified why you care about the idea, and why you're the best person to communicate a specific idea, you need to think about what you want to happen as a result of such communication. This is the "Solutions" part of Solutions-Oriented Ideas. There are several possible responses you could be aiming for. They can be grouped loosely under Understanding, Agreement, and Action.

Understanding

Sometimes it might be enough for someone else to just better understand you, your point of view, your organization's aims and purposes, or your company's offerings. Communicating a given idea or point of view is necessary to build a foundation for further understanding, agreement, or action. But right now, nothing more is needed. They just need to understand, not necessarily agree with you—or act. More often than not, however, understanding is a step toward agreement.

Agreement

Maybe you want someone to not just understand your point of view, but to agree with you. You want them to understand your idea and agree with it, to think it's a good idea, or to consider it the appropriate or correct approach to a challenge or problem. You want them to hold the same point of view as you. That agreement can still be considered foundational; it's necessary for future action, perhaps, but no action is needed right now. Yet, more often than not, agreement is a step toward action.

Action

Most of the time, however, we communicate ideas with other people hoping that they'll *do* something, or take action. That will certainly be the case in most business, sales, or marketing settings. If you want someone to do something once they've been exposed to an idea, it's helpful to know what action you want them to take.

For example, let's imagine that you work for a political nonprofit that is involved in community organizing, increasing issue awareness, legal support and advocacy, communicating with legislators, and otherwise working to affect the votes of citizens and legislators. When you staff the table at a community fair, what do you want the people who stop by the booth to talk with you to do?

They could perhaps sign a petition, sign up as a volunteer, take an information sheet or flier for an upcoming town hall meeting, sign up for your email mailing list, buy a T-shirt, or otherwise make a donation. Which action is most important? Which action is your highest priority? The next highest? Which action will have the most impact? Give thought to what actions you'd like them to take, prioritize those actions, and focus on directing them to the most compelling, effective action. In marketing, this is called a Call to Action.

Such actions can be grouped in several categories or types of actions:

Change in Behavior

You might want someone to start a new habit or otherwise change their behavior. Such an action might require communicating more than just your idea, but also why their current behavior or habit is suboptimal or less desirable, why your recommended behavior is better, and perhaps even ways that they can more easily adopt new behaviors in pursuit of the better habit or pattern of behavior.

Persuading Someone Else

Perhaps you want somebody to carry your idea to someone else, becoming a *carrier* of your idea virus, in a way. That could lead you to take additional steps, too, discussing the idea in ways that are more easily remembered so people are more likely to use those terms and words when discussing the topic or idea with someone else. You might also develop talking points or recommended ways to approach and address specific aspects of the subject matter. What are the key points you want someone to help pass on? In organized religion, this is represented in a way by apologetics, the practice of defending a religion through argument and discussion.

Deciding to Help You

This might be my favorite possible action, because help can come in so many different forms. For many readers of this book, this might be the response and action you desire most. Someone could help you by introducing you to someone else who might be able to help you with talent, resources, and other support. They might be able to offer financial assistance, support, and investment. They might be interested in working with you or for you. They could even recommend suppliers, distributors, and other potential business partners or services.

As you read this book, consider how I might be able to help you further develop and communicate your idea. Are you interested in coaching or consulting? Would you like to consider a speaking engagement, training session, or workshop for your team? Would you like to join a mastermind group with like-minded professionals? Let me know how I can help you.

Buying Something

This is the obvious one. If you're selling anything—a book, a T-shirt, skin care lotions and creams, Yu-Gi-Oh collectible trading cards, or professional services—it's clear that your preferred action in response to your communication would be a sale: your audience buying whatever it is you're selling. That's when communicating ideas gets the closest and most similar to sales. Dan Pink would even contend that we're all in sales, whether we like it or not.

Once you know what you want another person to do once you've communicated with them, you can turn your attention to them personally in the next section of this chapter.

A Question for You

What do you want people to do as a response to your communication and idea? What is your most important Call to Action? What is the singular Ask you'll focus on?

_____

_____

_____

_____

_____

How will your community, team, or organization benefit if others adopt the idea?

_____

_____

_____

_____

_____

What's in It for Me?

Now that you know why you're well suited to communicate about the idea—and you've determined what you want people to *do* after they've been exposed to the idea—you can turn your attention to the other person, people, or audience for your idea. What's in it for *them*?

Why does your idea matter to someone else? We've already explored why it matters to you. This question will help you better understand whether—and how—someone else would benefit from being exposed to your idea, as well as how receptive they might be to your idea. Has your potential audience shown interest in a similar idea, project, topic, or theme previously? (Think about how search and online ads react to our use of search engines and Web sites by way of behavioral targeting.) Do their current work, hobbies, or activities suggest that they are interested in what you have to offer? Do they have a question, experience a problem, or face a challenge that could be addressed by the idea you're developing? Or perhaps they just like you and are interested in knowing more about what you care about, what interests you, and what you're working on. (That could totally be true!)

Those are all examples of how you can consider why someone would care about your idea, not just why you would approach someone with or about your idea.

A Question for You

Why should your potential audience listen to you?

_____

_____

_____

_____

How does your idea connect with their life situation, experience, and needs?

_____

_____

_____

_____

_____

What will your idea do for them? What's in it for them?

_____

_____

_____

_____

_____

The Value Proposition

Once you clearly understand why you're trying to pursue an idea—
what's in it for you—and once you've identified what you want someone else to do once you've communicated the idea to them, you should
take some time to develop some reasons they should take those actions,
or accept and embrace the idea.

We can consider or call such reasons the value proposition or value
propositions. In product development and marketing, value propositions translate a product or service's features and functionality—similar
to the characteristics or aspects of an idea—into benefits for a person
who chooses to use that product or service.

Value propositions move beyond what an idea, product, or feature
does, toward what they can do for your audience.

A Question for You

What can your idea help your audience do or accomplish?

_____

_____

_____

_____

_____

What can your audience achieve if they adopt your idea?

_____

_____

_____

_____

What does your idea make easier or improve?

_____

_____

_____

_____

_____

The Offer

Admittedly, this is where the book—and the process—gets even more sales-y. There's much more that can be said about communicating ideas from a sales point of view in terms of unique selling propositions, sales pitches, elevator pitches, and so forth. Truth be told, at its core, sales itself is communication, specifically communicating ideas.

If you'd like to explore sales methods further with me, let me know, but for the purposes of this book, we can consider the offer in the following context. The offer is basically your idea presented with a little more polish but not yet the full package, positioned as a solution to a problem. (We'll return to the Pitch itself in Section 5.)

To develop your offer at this stage in the process, consider yourself as the ideal—or situational, in some cases—communicator, and consider the person you're going to communicate with as someone who will benefit from your idea's value proposition. You are offering them your idea as the solution to a problem, question, or challenge they face or have. You are approaching them as someone who will benefit from your idea.

From that point of view, your offer is you specifically bringing the idea to them—as part of a relationship, process, system, or package. You're not just communicating the idea as a disinterested party or disconnected agent—your presence or involvement is in some way part of the idea. You are offering them an opportunity.

A Question for You

What is your idea's value proposition? What will it do for the person you're communicating with? What problem or challenge will it help them overcome?

_____

_____

What is your offer to the person you're communicating with? What
do you propose the two of you do together?

_____

_____

_____

_____

What opportunity are you offering them?

_____

_____

_____

_____

Next Steps

Don't just leave it at that, though. Always have some next steps—
some recommended actions—lined up, ready, and able to suggest or
request. If you have a sales process, make sure to keep your audience
progressing through that process or whatever funnel you've established
for new customers. You might already have a sense of what the next

steps are. Consider our exploration of "What Do You Want?" above. In that section, you considered whether you wanted understanding, agreement, or action.

Use those three aspects to contextualize, develop, and frame your next steps, if you don't already have an explicit sales process. But don't just list things in mind for the person to do, prioritize those next steps, sequence them—and when communicating, tell them what the possible next steps are and help them take whatever next step makes sense given the situation. If no steps are immediately taken, even if you've offered a Plan A, B, and C, leave them with a reminder—and follow up in a couple of days to check in—or they might forget what they were going to do.

Similarly, if you get someone on board with an idea and then offer nothing else for them to do, that can lead you to miss or weaken your opportunity. Always have something for your audience to do next.

A Question for You

List two or three immediate next steps you would propose—and follow up on—based on your value proposition and offer.

_____

_____

_____

_____

_____

You have now completed Step 2, "Land on an Ask"—and determined your Ask. In the next chapter, you'll take the next step: you'll begin to craft what you choose to communicate *about* your idea.

Communicating My Ideas Case Study #1:
Scouts Eagle Project

As a youth in Wisconsin, I was actively involved in Cub Scouts and later Boy Scouts (now Scouts BSA, and welcoming young women as members). I loved the outdoor activities, the camping, and the hiking. I was a member of the Order of the Arrow, Scouting's honorary service organization; worked one summer at a local Scout camp; and went to two National Boy Scout Jamborees.

When I was 16, I earned the Eagle Award, the highest rank and recognition available in Scouts. That was the result of years of leadership and outdoor skills development. And to give back to the Scouting community, I still serve as a leader of the troop and district in which my son is active.

Working toward my Eagle involved an Eagle Project, perhaps the second large, memorable, challenging project I had ever worked on. It was definitely the largest and most challenging project I had worked on by that age. And it was a crash course in communicating ideas.

My project was leading Scouts from my troop in building a directional sign, a glass-encased bulletin board sign, and a handful of picnic tables for a rest stop along the Glacial Drumlin State Trail, a multipurpose rail trail in the Wisconsin State Park System. I partnered with a representative of a nearby Department of Natural Resources office to help with the project and secure the necessary approvals and materials. It was one of my first experiences interacting with a government employee with purpose as a youth.

That experience was challenging, and I was often nervous calling the DNR employee on the phone, working with him on the project, and stopping by the office or warehouse facility to assess and pick up materials for the project. We also had to agree on the details of the project, which involved various documents and materials lists. The more I worked with him, the more confident and competent I became, and our communication became easier. The more involved I got in the project, the more I had a firm grasp of its details and opportunities, and our collaboration improved to the point that I was truly managing the project myself—even as a youth.

I also had to communicate the idea to adults serving on the troop committee, preparing and presenting a project proposal and plan to be approved by the Scoutmaster, the committee chair, and a district representative who wasn't involved in the local troop. That involved additional communication, as well as fielding questions and concerns about the project.

Managing the project itself with Scouts from my troop was also challenging and involved active communication. I had to communicate not just what we had to do for the project—and how—but why it was important, why I wanted to do it, and what impact it would have on the rest stop, trail system, and bicyclists and other area residents. I had to promote the work days and make sure I had adequate volunteers on hand to do the necessary work. When things were done incorrectly, I had to instruct them on improvements and refinements—and I had to make sure that everyone had fun, too.

When I was all done with the project and the other requirements for Eagle, I defended my Eagle application in front of a district board of review involving adults from outside my local community and troop. That, too, required communication, not just about my project and the problem it solved, but my entire Scout experience, what I had learned, why it mattered to me, and how I'd apply it in the future.

All of that communication required major preparation and practice, and I learned several things. First of all, there's a first time for everything. For every idea, there will be the first time you communicate it to an audience. That might be daunting, but you can do it, and it can go well. Even if it doesn't, the next time you communicate the idea will be easier and less daunting, and you'll gradually become a more effective communicator.

Secondly, I learned that some audiences can be more open to your idea and more friendly to receive it than others. I don't remember any audience being particularly challenging, but I remember some audiences feeling higher stakes than others—perhaps the proposal or plan, and the board of review—representing a range of receptivity and understanding, and of acceptance. Not all audiences are equal, and it's important to identify a target audience that is predisposed toward your idea.

I also learned that your audience might sometimes include people you don't know at all, about whom you know nothing—and that they can still be receptive to your idea if communicated well.

Luckily, Scouting is a safe place for youth to share ideas, take risks, and pursue opportunities and adventures. I learned a lot communicating my idea to the various audiences, and last time I visited, at least one of the signs we built is still located at the rest stop along the Glacial Drumlin State Trail, in Sullivan, Wisconsin.

That's a long-lasting idea.

Section 2
Package

"We don't bring the product to the consumer, we bring the consumer to the product."

— DIETRICH MATESCHITZ, BUSINESS PERSON

One of the first and most compelling communication models I encountered as a professional and volunteer was Aristotle's model of communication. Not only was I delighted that people have been seriously and strategically considering this topic and process dating back almost 2,500 years ago (Aristotle died in 322 B.C.), the model still holds up pretty well.

Aristotle's model considers five primary elements that play a role in communication: the speaker, speech, occasion, audience, and effect. His approach to communications was relatively one way and unidirectional—the model's primary flaw—but is still informative.

You can visualize communication as occurring when a speaker hands the speech or communications object—I like to visualize a present or gift-wrapped box, complete with ribbon or bow—to the audience, on a given occasion, with a specific effect in mind. You might be able to draw the parallels to the 11-step process outlined in the Table of Contents.

In this section, we will consider what Aristotle would have considered speech. I consider it the communications object, in whatever form it might take: verbal or spoken; printed, online or offline; text, audio, or video. It is the package the communicator offers the audience.

This section and the two steps it contains will help you consider, create, and craft that Package.

Step 3
Keep It Simple

"Ideas are easy. Implementation is hard."

— GUY KAWASAKI, MARKETER AND VENTURE CAPITALIST

Collect Essential Information

Before you're able to communicate an idea, it's important to identify just what the idea is, and what you want—or need—to communicate about it. A further simplified version of Aristotle's model of communication might even include three parts: the sender, the communication itself, and the receiver. In Section 3, Person, we will focus on the sender, or you as the communicator specifically. In Section 4, Plan, we'll spend more time considering the receiver, or your audience. It is in this section, then, that we focus on what you are communicating, what you as the sender are giving the receiver: the Package.

Before you can actually figure out what the Package is going to be, you have to have something that you can make or mold into that package. When you start exploring and figuring out what you're going to communicate, think big. You want to start with as much as you can reasonably gather or start with, so at the end, you have winnowed it down to the bare essentials and the most important aspects and elements.

At the beginning, then, gather and collect any essential information—or *available* information, even—about the idea you'd like to communicate. In some cases, you might have a creative brief. You might have a project plan or technical specs. You might have the results of customer surveys or other marketing research. You might even have a description of the place you'd like to go—perhaps the outcome of a previous, similar effort. Or you might have a rough sketch depicting the physical item, object, or project; a Web site wireframe; or a mockup or design for your print collateral. Whatever it is, gather it.

At this stage of the process, we're not weeding things out yet, so try to gather as much as you possibly can. Sometimes, doing so might indicate that you don't know a lot, that there are remaining unanswered questions, or that there's something you need to further explore or expand on. That's OK. Sometimes preparing and planning indicates you need additional preparation and planning. That is very useful to learn, and early on is when you want to learn that—not once you're actually talking to someone about your concept or idea. Then, it's too late.

However, it's also possible to gather too much information—or to become paralyzed, worried that you have to collect everything or can't possibly collect everything—so feel free to set some false constraints on yourself as part of the collection exercise. You can approach that like a literature review, if it's helpful. Tell yourself things like: I'm only going to gather information from this year. I'm only going to consider documents from the product development team. I'm only going to use papers published in academic journals. I'm only going to incorporate information from venture capitalist blogs.

Those examples are arbitrary. The point is that you should collect as much information as you possibly can, and if doing so becomes unwieldy, overly daunting, or otherwise problematic, you can apply some constraints to make the task more manageable—and still make sense.

One thing you don't want to do at this stage is to start *excluding* information for reasons beyond whatever false constraints you set up to keep the task manageable. You are not making quality judgments right now, only quantity judgments. You are also not deciding that something isn't important or worth including. That will come later.

Right now, you are gathering anything and everything that might help identify gaps you need to explore and address, and that might help inform your approach to communicating your idea. This is an expansive exercise, not a convergent or optimizing exercise.

A Question for You

What information do you need to gather to plan your communication?

_____

_____

_____

_____

_____

Do you know where to get that information, readily? What sources, people, teams, or organizations will you draw on?

_____

_____

_____

_____

Are you missing any information? Do you need to remove any unnecessary information?

_____

_____

_____

_____

_____

Break It Down

Once you've gathered all of the information that you'd like to communicate with someone, you need to converge, optimize, and simplify that set. Otherwise, the other person will be overwhelmed and not know how to start making sense—neither heads nor tails!—of what you've just given them. So consider the material and information you've gathered, and begin to move it around. Group items that are similar, developing buckets or categories to contain them, perhaps even considering themes or meta-topics that can contain that content.

If you find that material is extremely, or even somewhat, dissimilar, check to make sure you don't have anything that's inconsistent or contradictory. And if you do, reconcile or resolve that contradiction. The last thing you want is a piece of isolated, stray information to undermine the consistency or credibility of what you're saying. And if something is dissimilar but not contradictory or untrue, consider why it's true. Make sure you have a story behind why the dissimilar information is relevant or true.

Break it down. When communicating, you might not end up sharing everything, unless you need to to answer questions or overcome objections. So give some thought to the overarching themes or meta-topics you've developed so they themselves make sense and are compelling. At this point, you can usually also determine what information isn't really necessary—so feel free to remove detail if it's not in service of communicating the value propositions, offer, and next steps you developed above in Step 2, "Land on an Ask."

A Question for You

When reviewing the information, do any themes or categories emerge?

_____

_____

_____

_____

_____

Does anything in particular seem problematic or suggest that it might require a story or side-explanation?

_____

_____

_____

_____

_____

Is there any information you can already identify as extraneous or unnecessary?

_____

_____

_____

_____

_____

Organize the Information

Once you've broken down the information you've gathered and grouped it into overarching themes or categories, give some additional thought to those categories. Look for patterns among those categories or themes. See if any suggested sequence of events or order emerges. If so, it'll be important that you present information in that order, to make the most sense and be most compelling.

That is particularly important if information is relevant because of other information, or if there's a series of events that's important to keep in mind when implementing your idea. Don't give the answer to a question or reason for something until other material you've covered inspires or prompts the question—or opens the opportunity for further explanation. If you do, your audience might become confused wondering why that information is important, and how it relates to what you've already told them. That could, in turn, lead them to develop questions about the validity of your idea, or to determine that the cost of your idea—however that's calculated—exceeds its benefit.

Be logical in your organization, either thematically or in terms of sequence, if there is one. The more sense you make in how you organize your categories, the easier it'll be to communicate your idea.

You might also find, in your experience of communicating your idea to others—or while practicing doing so—that you learn that a certain sequence or order of information is more effective than another sequence. If that's the case, go with what works. Take advantage of whatever sequencing best serves clarity and the attainment of your goals, whatever they are. Learn from experience. You can always change the sequencing again if a better order presents itself as effective.

A Question for You

Does it matter what order you present your information in?

_____

_____

Is any of the information dependent on other information?

Have you found that a particular order or sequence proves more effective? Why do you think that is?

Use Clear Language

Once you've broken down the information you gathered, and organized it into a logical order that works well with other people—the sequencing itself makes sense—go over what you plan to say, present, or convey (and the information you plan to share) for a clarity check. If your idea is technical, or if it requires any professional or other knowledge to understand, you might need to simplify it, depending on the audience. That is especially true if your audience also isn't technical or professional. Simplify your language so the non-technical or -professional person can easily understand what you're saying. Of course, the degree to which you do this will be dependent on your target audience, which we'll address in Step 7 below, "Take Aim." You might want to increase the technical or professional content in your communication, if that works well for that audience. But sometimes, even if your target is technical or professional, using more simple language can be useful.

In some cases, you might be talking to a mixed audience. Even if the more technical person is the decision maker, you'll want everyone to understand your message because everyone's opinion and point of view can affect or contribute to that person's decision. You'll have to determine what approach to take on a case-by-case basis. Be prepared to back up less-technical sharing of information with more technical details should the need arise.

Generally, however, you should plan to use everyday language. No acronyms, jargon, lingo, or slang, unless absolutely necessary. (As I like to say sometimes, "Slang is just lingo for jargon.") Don't assume or presume that others know what you know, or call things what you call them—especially outside your immediate team or organization. Use commonly used terms and everyday language so you don't have to further explain what you mean.

A Question for You

Are there any technical or professional terms or concepts you need to simplify?

_____

_____

_____

Do you know enough about your audience to determine whether the language you're using is appropriate for them?

_____

_____

_____

_____

_____

If you're communicating with a mixed audience, can you find a middle way that's appropriate for everyone?

_____

_____

_____

_____

_____

Eye the Design

Similarly, _how_ you present the information can also be important. That will vary situation to situation, but if the person you're planning to communicate with needs more clearly designed or highly polished material, be sure that how you present your information isn't a barrier to understanding, acceptance, or action. It can go in the other direction, however, as well. If you're trying to come off as grassroots or do-it-yourself, something that looks too nice, polished, or professional can work against that impression. So tailor the design to the audience.

For example, in my own work at Google, I have some colleagues and stakeholders who can see through the mess of something in development and process—to the idea inside. Other colleagues and stakeholders can't see beyond the formatting of a document or the refined polish or shine of a design. If something doesn't look ready for the public, they can't even get to the concept behind the communication piece. So I need to pay attention to how clean and clear even draft documents are when sharing with those various stakeholders, based on what they need to see and understand what I'm working on, as well as what I need from them at any given point in time. (That is not uncommon in writing and design, as well as in film and TV editing and production. Some people can handle drafts. Some people can only handle finals.)

That said, the more important thing to consider is whether the design—however polished or DIY it might be—helps you communicate what you're trying to communicate. Sometimes, a design—if it's too busy or complicated—can make communication challenging. Just like I recommend using simple language, I usually recommend simple design, too.

Don't try to be too fancy—or to include everything you want to communicate in a printed or online piece that you plan to leave behind or refer someone to. Just include the most important or most compelling information, and clear indicators of the next steps you identified above in Step 2, "Land on an Ask." Design the piece so it's part of your sales or communications process or funnel—so it helps someone take the next steps you'd like them to take. If you give them too much information or too many next steps, they might not retain or act on anything.

A Question for You

Do you need to design anything, either a printed piece to leave behind, or online material to refer them to?

_____

_____

_____

_____

Do you know whether your audience cares about design or has any expectations in terms of how your material is presented?

_____

_____

_____

_____

Do any internal colleagues or stakeholders have specific requirements in terms of draft vs. final?

_____

_____

_____

Get Feedback

It will be useful to practice before you actually communicate with someone. We'll touch on that in greater detail in Step 8 below, "Be Prepared." Run through what you want to communicate with a helpful partner, colleague, or friend. Do so before communicating with your audience. And ask for feedback.

In fact, you can seek feedback now. Bounce the current state of your information gathering, organization, clarity, and design—if you need to design something—off a partner, colleague, or friend. Get their comments, feedback, and input. Then, act on that feedback. Incorporate changes into your material.

Do so for any presentation outlines, talking points, presentation slides, and anything else you've had designed. It's very helpful to do so before using it with a more formal or actual audience.

That feedback and those improvements will help you communicate better. You'll have already gone through the material at least once—perhaps more than once. You, yourself, will be more comfortable.

A Question for You

When you shared your material, presentation outlines, and other draft documents with someone else, what feedback did you get?

What changes did you make as a result?

_____

_____

_____

_____

_____

Did their feedback give you any additional ideas?

_____

_____

_____

_____

You have now completed Step 3, "Keep It Simple"—gathered, organized, refined, and clarified the information you want to communicate. You've also taken a pass at designing any takeaways or leave-behinds that need to be designed. And you've gotten feedback from a team member or colleague. In the next chapter, you'll take the next step: Apply some polish and shine—some gloss—to what you plan to communicate.

Step 4
Seek the Shine

"Don't bother just to be better than your contemporaries or predecessors. Try to be better than yourself."

—WILLIAM FAULKNER, AUTHOR

At this stage in the *Communicating Ideas* process, you've spent quite a bit of time focusing on your Purpose—what your idea is and what you want the people you're reaching out to to do with it—as well as your Package—gathering the pieces, parts, information, and detail you want to communicate, and keeping it as simple as possible as you do so. You cannot communicate everything to everyone. Concentrate on the most important aspects of your idea, specific to the audience, people, and teams with which you'll be communicating.

In this step, you'll continue to focus on the Package of your idea—what you want to communicate. You'll also turn your attention to detail work. You'll sand down the rough edges. You'll smooth any sharp corners. You'll polish to attain a high-gloss shine. And you'll do your final quality assurance checks to be sure that the Package is appropriate for the audience you plan to target.

Be Different

In Step 1 above, "Start with an Idea," you considered the importance of an idea being different from other ideas for it to be a good idea. Take a moment now that you've gathered and digested all of the information related to your idea to reconsider whether your idea is clearly and explicitly different from other, related, or similar ideas. The last thing you want to do is to cover already well-traveled ground; only remind other people of other ideas, products, or services; or otherwise confuse people because they think someone came up with the idea—not you.

At the same time, reconsider now whether it's clear how your idea is different from others, if there are similar ideas already being considered or discussed by the public or your industry, profession, or community. Is the point—or are the points—of differentiation obvious, clear, and understandable? Is your idea different enough to stand out and be preferred over other ideas and competition in terms of mind share? Is that difference meaningful?

However, it's important to not obsess over competitors too much. Jaime Schmidt, founder of natural personal care company, Schmidt's Naturals, warns against attention to competitors keeping you from your own work and innovation. Focusing on competitors alone can keep you from moving beyond what is currently known. Regardless, it's still important and helpful to understand how your idea is different from others.

In marketing, professionals talk about this in terms of positioning. How is your product or service positioned in relationship to others in the marketplace? You'll spend more time exploring that in Step 5, "Become a Believer," below.

For now, if you don't think your idea is adequately different, there are two approaches to solving the problem. First of all, you can start by looking at how you're currently communicating. Don't go back to the original idea at this point. You might be able to clarify things merely in how you plan to communicate the idea. The idea itself might be fine. The challenge might be that how you are communicating or talking about the idea doesn't adequately capture and carry that difference.

However, in some cases, you might have to reconsider the idea itself. That usually takes more work, time, and effort because you're going back to root causes and actually changing the idea, not just changing your approach to communicating it, or about it and its benefits. But now is the time to do so—not later. If you need to change or improve on your idea in order to adequately communicate difference and a better or higher quality, do so now.

Hopefully, though, it's just a Package issue, not a Purpose issue. Regardless, if you do identify challenges with your purpose, definitely take on that work, as well, now. Do not try to solve problems with your idea by adjusting how you communicate.

Make sure your idea is strong—and meaningfully different—to begin with.

A Question for You

Is your idea adequately different from competing ideas?

_____

_____

_____

_____

_____

If not, is it a matter of packaging and communication, or do you need to return to the idea itself to improve its difference and uniqueness?

_____

_____

_____

_____

_____

Be Better

One of the best and most successful ways to be different is to be better. (Revisit Step 1, "Start with an Idea," if you'd like to review that.) What business person or leader doesn't want to be better than someone else at a skill, practice, trade, or profession? What organization or company doesn't want to offer the better program, product, or service? What innovator or sales person doesn't want to offer or provide a solution to a problem that is better than other existing solutions?

In fact, sometimes, being better is difference enough. Even if an idea, product, or service is similar to another, if it is demonstrably *better*, that difference in quality might be enough to make it stand out among competitive offerings.

There are multiple ways an idea can be better, and this stage in the process is a good time to determine whether and how your idea's higher or better quality might make it even sufficiently different in the minds of those you plan to communicate with. Is your idea easier or simpler? Does it take less effort, time, or work? Does it cost less? Are you able to implement it by yourself, with a small team, or with a larger group? Is it easier to explain to other people? Does a process have fewer steps? Have people responded well to similar ideas in the past?

All of those might be useful questions to inspire potential positioning statements as you consider this aspect of the package of your idea. Another way to approach this is as follows: List all of the differences between your idea and similar or competing ideas. Then, for each difference, indicate whether it is a benefit for a given idea, or a liability for that idea—when compared to the competing idea. That can be a useful way to determine whether differences can lead to clear and evident ways in which an idea is demonstrably better because of its differences.

A Question for You

Is your idea better than competing ideas?

_____

_____

_____

_____

As you consider how your idea is different and better than other ideas, what are some definable positioning statements you could consider using to communicate how your idea compares to others?

_____

_____

_____

_____

_____

Deliver Value

One way that an idea, practice, process, product, or service can be different from or better than another is that it costs less... or is worth more. You don't have to think about value in purely monetary terms, but consider—or reconsider—just what value is offered or provided by your idea. In Step 2 above, "Land on an Ask," you noted a few value propositions that might be useful at this stage. How will you communicate your idea's value propositions to clearly communicate its value to your target audience?

Does your idea actually matter? Is it a need to have, or a nice to have? How much impact could your idea have on someone's life or life experience? If you can quantify the idea's value, merit, or impact, all the better. But it's OK if you cannot—as long as you're able to indicate clearly and capably why the idea matters, and what it will do: its value proposition.

Another interesting way to consider and communicate value is to consider what else an idea connects to or with—or can draw on in terms of your personal, team, and organizational capabilities, activities, goals, and characteristics. Does an idea—a church youth group lock in, for example—help the group use up refreshments and table service items acquired for a past event that was canceled or perhaps didn't attract as many participants as expected? Does a proposed hike itinerary take you and your partner to a part of the state that's also known for its wineries and B&Bs—so you can also scope out future weekend trip destinations? Does a specific movie feature a cast member you know your friend is particularly fond of?

One way to think about that connection is in terms of multipliers. Just like calling a relative while going on a walk around the block or in the neighborhood helps you use time effectively by combining two activities, applying multipliers to how you communicate ideas and how you consider the value of your idea can also be productive.

A Question for You

What value propositions did you identify in Step 2, "Land on an Ask"?

_____

_____

_____

_____

_____

Are those value propositions still relevant and useful given the packaging work you've now done?

_____

_____

_____

_____

_____

Can you quantify the value or impact of your idea? How so? What's it worth?

_____

_____

_____

_____

Are there any multipliers you can consider along with your idea?

_____

_____

_____

_____

Cost Less than It's Worth

Let's spend a little more time thinking about value. As above, you don't have to think about value in purely monetary terms. This isn't necessarily about being less expensive than an alternative option. It's about making sure that the value equation is clearly and easily recognized and understood by the people you're communicating with. As you explored in Step 2, "Land on an Ask," and reaffirmed above, you can consider your idea's value propositions.

At the same time, your audience will be doing some math of their own. You can get ahead of that. Think through what costs, barriers, or downside might exist for your idea—perhaps framing them as objections people might raise—as well as the benefits, bridges, and upside that also exist. You want to be fully able to understand whether—and how—the upside outweighs any downside, so you can better communicate about any trade offs or need to balance to others.

If it turns out that the costs actually outweigh the benefits, you have a couple of options. You can either be totally open, honest, and transparent about that—and take that hit in perception, preference, and uptake. You can also go back to the idea and rework it so the benefits eventually overcome and overtake any costs. That—obviously—is the ideal situation, but sometimes you don't have the luxury at this stage in the process.

If your idea's costs are greater than its benefits—in effect, a negative value—it might not be impossible to persuade someone that your idea has merit. It'll certainly be more challenging. One way you can address that is by adding additional customer service or support, throwing in other items as bonuses, or otherwise trying to add more value to the package of your idea.

A Question for You

Does the value of your idea outweigh its costs? Are you able to communicate that clearly?

_____

_____

_____

_____

If your idea's costs outweigh its value, how will you address that? Will you (a) improve the idea to increase its value and lower its costs, (b) add additional service or support, (c) throw in additional products or ideas, or (d) do something else?

_____

_____

_____

_____

_____

How will doing so affect how you communicate about your idea?

_____

_____

_____

_____

_____

Be Realistic

In Step 1, "Start with an Idea," one of the hallmarks of a good idea was that the idea was "doable." I don't think that adequately communicates what we can best communicate about our ideas in terms of value propositions and potential value to our audience. Even "feasibility" doesn't entirely capture our goal here, so I'd like you to think about it in terms of being *realistic*.

How realistic is your idea? How realistic is the concept of your audience implementing your idea? Explore just how reasonable, possible, probable, or likely your idea is to be received—and implemented—by the audience with which you're going to communicate. Does your idea make sense for them?

One way to approach how realistic your idea is, is to apply a "sniff test" or a "stink test." Is there anything at this stage or phase of your communications planning that doesn't seem right, that seems off, or that... smells bad or stinks? This is a totally subjective, gut-level way to consider your idea and communications plan, to seek a reality check—so far focusing on your Purpose and Package.

You might also consider having someone else apply a sniff test or a stink test at this stage—another form of seeking feedback. Is it clear that the value is greater than the cost? Does the packaging seem right and reasonable for the audience? Does anything stand out as confusing or contradictory? Sometimes the stink test—or reality check—can identify or uncover design flaws or issues you might have missed otherwise.

Take a moment, pause, and sniff around a little. How does your idea smell? Does it pass the stink test?

A Question for You

Is it realistic that your audience understands, accepts, and implements your idea?

_____

_____

_____

_____

_____

Does a team member, colleague, or friend also think that your idea is realistic?

_____

_____

_____

_____

_____

Does anything seem off about the idea or how you plan to communicate about it?

_____

_____

_____

_____

_____

How do you plan to address any aspects that seem unrealistic?

_____

Wrap the Gift

You are now almost done with the packaging of your idea and the message you intend to communicate to your audience. Let's return now to visualizing your idea as a package or box passed between the speaker—the communicator—and the listener, or receiver. What kind of box is it? How big is it? Do you need to do anything more to that box before giving it to someone else?

Take the package metaphor further. It's a present. How will you wrap that box? Depending on your idea and the intended audience, there are a number of approaches—just like when gift wrapping an actual present. You might find that the personal approach is best: newspaper or rough brown wrapping paper and twine, perhaps even electrical tape or duct tape. Label it with a Sharpie by hand. Or, you might find that a more professional approach is best: expensive, high-gloss wrapping paper, edges and lines tight and straight, tape tidy, and ribbons or bows primly and perfectly curled. And sometimes, without wrapping paper of any kind works, too.

Metaphor aside, give thought now to any final touches you'd like to put on your idea's Package. You can go as is, rough it up a little for a more homey, grassroots feel, or aim for high gloss and glam. You might also find that there are additional items you want to put in the package before you hand it to your audience. Or, you might want to remove something. It all depends on you, your idea, and your chosen audience—and what works for that communications combination.

Even if you choose not to wrap the gift, you'll have done so strategically, and fully consciously.

A Question for You

Is your idea package ready to hand to your audience? Will it be more effective to be informal, or to be totally buttoned-up and professional?

_____

_____

_____

_____

As you think more about your idea and its packaging, is there anything else you need to add, or remove?

_____

_____

_____

_____

You have now completed Step 4, "Seek the Shine"—and applied some gloss to the packaging of your idea, putting a ribbon and bow on the present you plan to offer your audience. In the next section, you'll shift from considering the Purpose (Section 1) and Package (Section 2) of your idea to you, the communicator, as a _Person_. In Section 3, I will give you advice and guidance on how to become a more persuasive advocate for your idea, and how to bring your best, most energetic self to your communication.

Communicating My Ideas Case Study #2:
The Company of Friends

In 1996, I joined the staff of *Fast Company* magazine. I had worked
for several weekly and daily newspapers, including the *San Francisco
Chronicle*, as well as two national magazines before joining the *Fast
Company* team. There, I was the 17th employee.

The primary job of journalists is communicating ideas. They talk
to people, and then they write about what they talked about—and
what they learned—to share those ideas more broadly. Journalists
also communicate ideas to each other to decide what articles to
write and include in the newspaper or magazine, or online. We
actually call them story ideas. Not all story ideas end up in print
or online. Not all stories get told, but with the advent of blogging,
social media, online video, and podcasting, more people can tell
each other more stories and communicate more ideas.

At *Fast Company*, we communicated more than one idea, and
not just in terms of story ideas. Different from other business magazines at the time, we didn't necessarily focus on CEOs and other
executives or business news. We concentrated on innovation and
leadership. We also focused on people making change in their organizations, industries, and communities regardless of their position
or title. And given that it was the onset of the New Economy, we
wrote about how business could be a positive force in the world
and how people could more successfully find personally meaningful
and rewarding work.

Those are all big ideas.

We also communicated the idea that magazines could help
people connect. We printed contact information for the people we
wrote about early in the magazine's history. (The magazine doesn't
do that any more.) We helped readers connect and discuss the ideas
addressed in the magazine in online discussion forums. We held
semi-annual RealTime conferences at which readers could mix and
mingle with the staff, the people we wrote about, and each other.

And before there was social media, we launched a readers network in which readers could meet in each other's homes, offices, and communities to discuss the ideas at a local level. Over the course of the history of the readers network, which remained active until I left the magazine in 2005, more than 45,000 readers joined local groups in about 165 cities and 30 countries around the world. That's small compared to the online social media of today, but at the time, an online-offline readers community was a big idea.

When I first communicated the idea of the readers network to co-founding editor Alan Webber, now the mayor of Santa Fe, New Mexico, I had a proof of concept. As editor of the weekly email newsletter *Fast Take*, I'd started including an item encouraging readers to write in if they wanted to meet other readers. I'd been manually maintaining a spreadsheet of names and contact information to copy and paste when emailing back to new members. Groups had already started gathering.

Alan was receptive to the idea. In fact, a reader had contacted him directly asking if there was a way to connect with and meet other readers in person. He gave his approval, and we formally launched the network, which was an amazing experience as a young journalist, marketer, and community organizer.

I learned a lot working on the Company of Friends. The idea might warrant a book all its own some day. But here, I'll call out a few things. One, the active communicating and sharing of ideas, leads to other, new ideas—and better ideas. When you bring people together and the object of exchange is ideas, ideas flourish. Two, sometimes ideas can be communicated by different sources and received from different angles, adding up to a larger idea. The fact that someone else had approached Alan with the idea in close proximity to my doing so made it an even bigger idea, and an idea more likely to land. And three, with 45,000 members, all leaders and innovators in their own right, there can be a lot of ideas. Communicating them all can be challenging, and a crowded marketplace of ideas can be noisy indeed. Regardless, with enough people, enough attention, and enough energy, all ideas can become real. You just need to find the right partners.

That's why I wrote this book: to help you learn how to better communicate your idea so it stands out and can succeed with the right partners.

Section 3
Person

"Don't follow the crowd. Let the crowd follow you."

—MARGARET THATCHER, POLITICIAN

In Section 2 above, Package, I introduced the concept of Aristotle's model of communication. To review briefly, in the simplified model, you can consider the basic elements as including a communicator, the idea being communicated—the Package we just explored fully—and the audience. In this section, we will consider you as the communicator, your *Person*.

By that, I don't necessarily mean *who* you are, per se. I will not address and we will not necessarily discuss who you are in terms of gender, race, age, or other personal characteristics or demographics. We will, however, explore *how* you are. The way you act, are, behave, and carry yourself can increase—or decrease—the likelihood of your audience receiving and responding to your idea well.

Because our attention is on *how* you are, rather than who you are, we will address a couple of things that you can do—that any communicator can do—to better communicate your ideas, personally.

Step 5
Become a Believer

"Jump, and you will find out how to unfold your wings as you fall."

— RAY BRADBURY, AUTHOR

You now know the Purpose of your idea—what it is, what you want people to do, and what you and your organization want to accomplish. You've also given thought to the Package of your idea—what your message is and how it'll be delivered, what it looks like, how it feels. Now it's time to step back and consider the Person who will carry that message, the person who will give the package to the receiver or audience. That communicator is you.

I don't intend to attempt any major makeover at this stage or step in the process. Regardless, if you'd like to learn more about additional steps you can take to become a better communicator, please don't hesitate to reach out to me. I have additional resources and tools to offer you.

For the sake of this step, you are who you are. You have a role that you'll fulfill as communicator of your given—or chosen—idea. In my decades of marketing, journalism, and training experience, I have encountered tens of thousands of people, teams, organizations, and ideas.

Not only were each of them different, but the synergy or connection between the people, teams, and organizations—and their ideas and innovations—were also different. Magic can happen when you bring the right people and the right ideas together—on the sending *and* receiving side. That's part of what makes communications so much fun. Regardless, you are who you are. And at this point, the idea is what it is. There are still things you can learn or do about yourself—to become a bigger and better believer in your idea.

What's in It for You? (Part Two)

In Step 2 above, "Land on an Ask," you considered the question "What's in it for you?" Review the notes you made above responding to the question prompts "Why do you care about this idea? Why are you the best person to communicate this idea?"

Next, return to the section "What's in It for Me?" in that same step and review the point of view of your audience. Consider the notes you made in reaction to the prompts "Why should your potential audience listen to you?", "How does your idea connect with their life situation, experience, and needs?", and "What will your idea do for them? What's in it for them?"

Taking into account the motivations of you as the communicator—and the motivations of your audience—reaffirm your personal motivation. Recommit to why you want to communicate your idea and to doing your best work in that role.

It might be the case that that is easier now that you know more about the Purpose behind the idea, as well as its overall Package. You now know more about why you're communicating about the idea, subject, or topic, and you also know more about what you'd like to communicate. That should give you additional information and inspiration to run with, and you might very well find yourself newly energized, inspired, and motivated. (If you're not, consider what additional motivation you might need, and seek it.)

In short, there should be more value and benefit evident to you as the communicator at this point in the process. If there isn't, you now know more about the Purpose and Package of your idea or concept—so you can better step up to the task even if you need a little extrinsic motivation. In the following section, Step 6, "Power Up," you will learn some of the additional and sometimes fun and exciting steps you can take to add some gloss and shine to *yourself* as a communicator, similar to what you did to the idea itself.

In this section, however, you'll continue to explore aspects of you personally as the communicator that can come into play.

A Question for You

Does the personal motivation you identified in Step 2, "Land on an Ask," still resonate for you? Do you need to restate it, refine it, or update it? (If so, do so below.)

_____

_____

_____

_____

_____

Does the motivation you documented above for your audience still resonate as accurate and appropriate? Do you need to restate it, refine it, or update it? (If so, do so below.)

_____

_____

_____

_____

_____

Do you need to increase or improve your motivation? What additional motivation do you want or need to bring your best self as the communicator to your idea?

Go Back to Basics

In Step 3 above, "Keep It Simple," we explored the importance of keeping an idea simple. People even use the acronym K.I.S.S.—Keep It Simple, Silly. As you consider yourself as the communicator and what you need to do your job well, it's now time to go back to the very basics of your idea and concept to ensure you fully understand it at the lowest foundation.

So far in *Communicating Ideas*, you started small, then expanded and improved what you plan to communicate. Now it's time to go back to basics and think small again to make sure you communicate the bare essentials and aren't distracted by some of the additional gloss and shine—and context—that you've been spending time with.

It's also a good opportunity for you to think ahead to how you will communicate what you'd like to address simply, easily, clearly, and cleanly. In fact, the less you need to do or say to get an idea across, the better—and the easier your job will be.

Start small—begin with the basics—and set everything else aside to address questions, mitigate concerns, and otherwise respond to objections, questions, and other feedback to the idea once you've presented it to your audience.

A Question for You

What are the most basic elements or aspects you want to communicate?

_____

_____

_____

_____

What details and information can you set aside for later?

_____

_____

_____

_____

Are you able to prioritize, rank order, or sequence the information for ideal delivery?

_____

_____

_____

_____

Dig Deep

Ironically, to be able to begin with the basics, or to go back to the basics at this stage, you also need to continue digging deep. As you prepare yourself to communicate efficiently and effectively, you want to balance preparing to communicate the lowest common denominator information about your idea—the basic essentials—with preparing to go deep, long, and wide as needed.

That doesn't just prepare you to share additional, more in-depth information beyond the basics or essentials. Though it does do that. Such depth also helps you reconsider the basics you plan to communicate. Focusing on the essentials while still considering the broader context can help you select the best information and material to convey given that context.

Focusing on the most critical parts as well as the whole can help prepare you as a communicator for the initial stages of an interaction, as well as later in the discussion or exchange. It can also help you confirm that you have the best content available to you at every stage of the process.

A Question for You

Can you see how the most important information serves as the nucleus of larger molecules of detail?

_____

_____

_____

_____

_____

As you consider your bare essentials while also considering the whole, do you need to change or update your approach?

_____

_____

_____

_____

Know Your Competition

You can generally consider your competition as people, teams, or companies that do something similar to what you and our organization does in terms of business, products, or services. In your role as a business person, maker, creator, community organizer, group leader, sales person, and other communicator, however, it's also important to consider the competition in terms of your ideas—and the specific idea about which you're communicating.

There might very well be competing concepts or ideas, solutions, events, proposals, products, or services that are similar to—or even just adjacent to—the idea you plan to communicate. Do your due diligence and understand those competitors. You don't have to learn everything about competing ideas, but you should at least understand the basics.

As a communicator, doing so is helpful in several ways. First of all, considering the competition for your idea can help you learn and know more about your own idea and topic of communication. You will better understand the context in which your idea exists—and therefore become a better communicator.

Secondly, understanding competing ideas will help you define and refine what you choose to communicate. If a competitive idea is relatively similar to your idea in one area, but your offering stands out in another, you can focus your attention on that aspect of the idea. (Return to the material on value propositions above. You'll learn more about positioning below.)

And thirdly, other options or choices—competing ideas—might arise in conversation and discussion with your audience once you're communicating. It behooves you as a communicator to be aware of other available options, and to be able to address them directly should they be mentioned. Understanding of your segment, category, or industry broadly—and being up to date on competing concepts and ideas—will increase your audience's estimation of you as a professional.

A Question for You

Are there any other relatively recent or current concepts, ideas, or solutions that can be seen as competition?

_____

_____

_____

_____

_____

What ideas compete with yours? Is that competition direct or indirect?

_____

_____

_____

_____

_____

Make a Difference

Once you've identified the competition for your idea, concept, service, product, or solution, you can consider and identify how your idea is different from—and better than—the other options. In marketing, this is called positioning, and there's quite a bit of art and science, as well as research, that goes into full positioning. But you can position your idea lightly here and now—for the purposes of your immediate communications needs—by considering the competitive offerings or options, and then considering how your idea is different.

You don't necessarily want to lead with or be the person to introduce this difference, or informal positioning, but you want to be prepared to address competitive options should they come up in conversation. Certainly, you want any differences that you highlight or address to position your idea as a better solution or idea than the competitors or alternatives. Do not dwell or focus on differences that indicate your idea is the lesser or lower quality of two options or offers.

You can also think about differentiation and positioning in terms of what the idea will do for your audience. (Similar to value propositions above.) What difference will the idea make? How will your idea solve a problem for them, improve their life, affect a situation, or make a task easier?

Difference can be considered in multiple ways: standing out from competitors in terms of positioning, but also focusing on the impact your idea will have that other potential solutions might not.

A Question for You

How are the competing ideas you identified similar to your idea? How are they different?

How can you differentiate or better position your idea given this new understanding of competing ideas?

What difference will your idea make for your audience?

Juice the Fruit

Finally, make sure you're having fun. It's OK to roll your sleeves up and get your hands dirty a little bit.

In fact I'd like you to do a little creative visualization. Picture, if you will, that your idea is an orange. It's a somewhat large orange, but it's not as big as a grapefruit. It has a bright orange peel, perhaps mottled in spots with darker orange. Now, I'd like you to imagine opening the orange. But don't peel the orange with an orange peeler. And don't break the skin with your teeth. How else could you open it? You could try to just pull at the peel with your fingers. Or you could just squeeze it. Push it around in your hands, or pull it apart, and feel the sudden spritz of juice from inside the peel. Imagine the juice on your palms, between your fingers, and on your wrists. Get your hands dirty.

Weird, huh? A little, maybe, if you're new to the idea. But fun, hopefully. (And if it wasn't, try it again sometime. Visualization and guided meditation that includes visualization can be a useful tool.) Sometimes communicating ideas can be like that brief visualization. Look for the dirty, messy parts of the idea, or of the process, and hold that in your mind. Or think about the sweet, tangy, citrus flavor of freshly squeezed orange juice and try to capture that energy and effervescence in what you communicate about the idea or how you communicate.

Regardless, throw yourself fully into the process as the communicator. Roll your sleeves up. Rub your palms together. And get busy having fun while you work.

A Question for You

What would you consider the "juice" of the idea? How can you communicate that juice to your audience?

You have now completed Step 5, "Become a Believer"—in which you've returned to your personal motivation as a communicator, pinpointed the bare essentials you want to communicate, considered the broader context around and behind those basics, identified competing ideas, homed in on how your idea is different and better, and accentuated the excitement and fun surrounding your idea.

In the next chapter, you'll take the next step, learning some tactics and tips that will help you be fully present, involved, and focused while in the act of communicating with your audience.

Step 6
Power Up

"Outstanding leaders go out of their way to boost the self-esteem of their personnel. If people believe in themselves, it's amazing what they can accomplish."

—SAM WALTON, BUSINESS PERSON

In the previous step, you focused on some things you will want to do as the communicator to ensure that you are bringing your whole self to the idea—as well as the whole idea to your audience. Now it's time to turn your attention—while still focusing on you as the communicator—to *how* you communicate.

Step 6, "Power Up," will offer guidance on the material and information you share, the importance of eye contact and body language, the need to pay attention to and respond to your audience, the value of persistence and perseverance, and the impact of a cheerful personality.

This step addresses what you need to do while you're actually communicating. You can adjust and improve your communication in real time on the fly to better meet the needs of your audience.

Knowledge Is Power

So much of the perceived quality of your communication is your confidence and competence. As Dr. John DeMartini once told me,

"Fluency is congruency." Your audience will judge the quality of your idea—and you as the purveyor of the idea—based on the quality of your communication. We've touched on that extensively above—you must know your idea inside and out. It is a requirement—table stakes, if you're a betting person—to be as fully informed and as fluent about your product, service, idea, and industry as you can possibly be. Gaps in knowledge can lead to surprises, as well as lesser successes.

Similarly, the impact of your idea—its potential effect on your audience—also depends on your confidence and competence as a communicator. Not only do you want to be fully informed about your idea, but you want to have a firm grasp on its context, as well. You just considered whether there are competitive options to your ideas. You explored how those competitors might relate and compare. And you've identified any special considerations that need to be made about any of the ideas, including your own.

And lastly, you want to know about your audience. Who are they? What do they need? How does your idea connect with them? You will spend more time with that in the next chapter, Step 7, "Take Aim."

A Question for You

Are you confident that you know everything you need to know about your idea?

_____

_____

_____

_____

_____

Are you confident that you know everything you need to know about your idea's context?

_____

_____

_____

_____

_____

Is there anything additional that you might not know that you don't know?

_____

_____

_____

_____

_____

Listen—and Look—Empathetically

Even though much of communications training focuses on the act of communication—on presenting, speaking, or writing—it's even more important to know when not to speak. More than half of communication is determined by listening, which is done by you, as well as your audience. When your audience responds, what do they say? Are their statements positive, neutral, or negative? What questions do they ask? What types of questions do they ask?

Even though what people say—and what you hear and understand—is important, you can also learn a lot by paying attention otherwise. Sometimes, unspoken reactions, responses, and cues communicate a lot—even more than what someone says. Is your audience paying attention while you talk with them? Where are they looking? Are they listening deadpan, looking to the side, or maintaining eye contact and nodding? When and where do they nod? Do they ever shake their head, furrow their brow, grimace or purse their lips, or give another negative physical reaction (or *tell*, if you're a betting person)?

Pay attention to your audience's facial expressions, body, and posture. If their body posture is open, arms and legs open—not crossed or in front of the body—they might feel at ease, comfortable, and safe. Similarly, if their body posture is closed, arms and legs crossed or in front of the body, they might feel attacked, defensive, or hostile. Such physical responses and body postures can also offer feedback as you communicate.

That can also be as easy as leaning in or reclining. If someone is leaning into you, or standing closer, they might be more engaged, involved, and open to your idea. If someone is reclining, moving away from you, or standing away from you, they might be less so.

A Question for You

Are you aware of your facial expressions and posture when speaking with others? Are you aware of your tone of voice and speaking pace?

_____

_____

_____

_____

_____

As you communicate with your audience, what do they say? What questions do they ask? And how do they respond physically in terms of facial expressions and body posture?

How can you change your communication style in response to such statements, questions, and physical reactions to your idea?

Think Critically

Don't just listen and pay attention, however, listen with intent. Give due consideration to what the members of your audience are saying, as well as how they're responding verbally and nonverbally otherwise. Consider their spoken and physical reactions and responses as feedback, input, and signals. Do they signal acceptance? Understanding? Questions? Disagreement? Rejection? Every signal has meaning.

   Adjust your communication in response as you go. That can be somewhat challenging at times. You might need to "smooth the curve" a little bit and not respond to every single reaction and response—look for the aggregate response from the individual, the sum of their signals. And similarly, when speaking to a larger group or audience, read the room, not individuals, necessarily. You can usually gauge and gather the majority of a group's response, even with a larger audience.

Home Depot co-founder Arthur Blank suggests that listening to customer concerns and needs can help you become more competitive. He and fellow co-founder Bernie Marcus used to station themselves outside Home Depot stores in order to talk with customers. Instead of spending more time with people who had bought something, Blank concentrated on the empty-handed people, to find out why they hadn't bought something. That proved more helpful in developing new ideas and solving problems than talking with satisfied customers.

Responding to such signals, even if dissatisfied, doesn't mean to lie or otherwise be dishonest, however. It doesn't mean that you misrepresent your idea, product, or service. But respond and react—in turn—with empathy, address concerns, answer questions, and change how you're communicating—as a communicator—to best reach the audience depending on their responses.

In addition, try to see things from the point of view of your audience, from their perspective. Don't drink so much Kool-Aid that you are unaware of or can't appreciate or recognize any flaws or limitations of your idea. Make sure that you communicate your idea in their terms—and in their interest. And remember that they have options, alternatives, and competing ideas available to them.

Finally, as you listen to your audience's feedback, objections, questions, and other responses, give full thought to your response—drawing on some of the topics we'll touch on later in the book—to be sure to adequately and appropriately address their concerns.

A Question for You

If you've communicated with this audience before, what kinds of questions do they usually ask? What are they normally concerned about or interested in?

_____

_____

_____

_____

_____

Are there things that they tend to like? Not like?

_____

_____

_____

_____

What do you need to do in order to take in, recognize, and respond to their vocal, facial, and physical reactions and responses?

_____

_____

_____

_____

What is the sum of the signals they're giving you in response to your idea? How can you best react and respond to those signals, in turn?

_____

_____

Patience and Perseverance

As you prepare yourself to communicate and to be the best communicator you can be, keep in mind that communication is not something you rush. It's not something you want to drag out interminably—that's one reason this book is relatively short (I could write a book about each step or section. If you'd like me to do so, let me know which sections are most important and interesting to you!) But you also want to take your time.

If you go into a communications situation or opportunity feeling agitated or impatient, wanting the exchange and interaction to go quickly—already wanting it to be over—your audience will totally pick up on that. Chances are that they'll interpret that as a lack of engagement, involvement, or investment in your idea as a communicator.

Try to remain fully present and engaged with your audience for the duration of your communication and time with them, however long that takes. Remember that communication doesn't only include what you plan to say or share in person or via other media; it also involves your audience's response and reaction, questions and feedback—and your response in kind. Communication is bidirectional, and occurs more than once. Give every moment your full attention and engagement. Be fully present. Give it your all.

At the same time, it's important to remember that you are also involved in this—supporting and advocating your idea—for the long haul. If at first you don't succeed, try, try again. Pick yourself up, dust yourself off, and start all over again. Learn from your previous experience, adjust your approach to that audience—that might be the most important part—and approach again at another time.

Likewise, if you don't succeed in communicating your idea to one audience, even after a period of patience and persistence, there are other audiences. Learn from your experience, adjust your approach as needed, and seek another audience. Don't just give up after one time, or just a few times. Keep trying.

A Question for You

Do you have enough time to dedicate to successfully communicating your idea? What do you need to do to make sure you have enough time to focus on that?

_____

_____

_____

_____

Can you commit to persist and persevere even if your audience doesn't accept or agree to your idea immediately?

_____

_____

_____

_____

Based on their initial reaction or response, what do you need to do to improve or adjust your communication for the next opportunity you have with them?

_____

_____

_____

_____

_____

What other audiences might be open to your idea?

_____

_____

_____

_____

Polish Your Personality

As a communicator, you will always want to be authentic and true to yourself. This is also an opportunity and an invitation to become or create a better self—to perhaps more successfully carry your message to others. As you communicate your message time and time again (patiently and persistently, as mentioned above), take note of and pay attention to where *you* get in your own way, and in the way of communicating your idea. Do you use slang phrases that get in the way? Do you laugh too loudly, throwing people off guard? Do you think you stand too close to the people you're talking to? Do you get nervous? Do you have bad breath?

Give thought to what you are like, how you carry yourself, and how you come across. That is a good opportunity to assess your speaking style, how formal or informal you are with people, how personal or professional you act, how you gesture, even what you wear. Take time right now to think about yourself as a package, too. Much like your idea is the package you plan to communicate—to hand to your audience—you as the communicator are *also* a package.

Now is the time to smooth any rough edges, to accentuate the positive you already bring, and to otherwise tidy up who you are as the communicator—in addition to tidying up your message, your idea, and what you communicate. You might even realize that you could benefit from and consider pursuing some kind of additional training. Public speaking, presentation skills, media training, or something else along those lines might be useful.

I can help identify useful books, programs, and other resources that you might find helpful in that regard. Just let me know what you'd like to learn more about.

A Question for You

Do you get in your own way sometimes when communicating? How so?

_____

_____

_____

_____

How would you prioritize the challenges you present yourself when communicating? What do you think you need to address first in order to become more successful?

_____

_____

What resources should you use to address those needs and challenges?

Bring Cheer

All of the above can be relatively challenging—especially patience and persistence, and sometimes, addressing our own personal, physical, and other characteristics. So far in this step, you've got to learn everything you can, listen really intently, think critically, be as patient and persistent as you can possibly be, and keep on your toes, always on your A game. I would also suggest—perhaps upping the ante—that you should always remain cheerful, too, and exude confidence.

Cheerfulness, and a good attitude, goes a long way. Not only does it help you do the work you need to do with your chosen audience in terms of communication and persuasion—cheer is more compelling than grumpiness—it makes your job easier and more fun, too. In Scouts BSA, the Order of the Arrow—Scouting's service organization—focuses on remaining cheerful "even in the midst of irksome tasks and weighty responsibilities." Cheer can help hard work feel lighter, so cheerfulness, positivity, and optimism will be helpful at a personal, individual level. Cheerfulness can also help improve the attitudes and relationships of the colleagues and coworkers around you during challenging times, as well. And it affects your audience, too. Cheerfulness, optimism, and positivity—a spirit of solving problems—will help you become a more compelling communicator. In his book *The Ideas Industry*, Daniel Drezner suggests that optimism and confidence are among the characteristics helping place thought leaders in better standing with mainstream audiences than traditional academics and public intellectuals in recent years. Your case will be better made with an attitude of cheer. You will be a better communicator if you remain cheerful.

A Question for You

To what extent are you able to remain cheerful, optimistic, and positive?

_____

_____

_____

_____

Do you find it challenging to communicate that attitude to others?

_____

_____

_____

_____

What are three things you can do to increase and improve your cheerfulness?

_____

_____

_____

_____

_____

You have now completed Step 6, "Power Up"—focusing on who you are and how you are while actively communicating with your audience. You've considered active listening, critical thinking, and your personality and physical presence while communicating.

In the next section and its two steps, you'll proceed from focusing on your idea as what you are going to communicate, how you are going to communicate it, and on yourself as the communicator—who you are and how you need to communicate—to your audience.

Communicating My Ideas Case Study #3:
Digital Storytelling Bootcamp

Early on in the history of the Company of Friends, I participated in a Digital Storytelling Festival and Bootcamp hosted by Dana Atchley in Crested Butte, Colorado. What I remember most is the Bootcamp, a brief, intense, small-group workshop on digital storytelling led by Joe Lambert and Nina Mullen. During the Bootcamp, you created your own digital story using late-1990s desktop video editing software. The idea was that you made your story at the Bootcamp, and then showed it at the Festival, which also featured other talks, activities, and screenings. The Festival was a larger audience conference associated with the more intimate workshop.

A multimedia storyteller and advocate since the 1970s, Atchley was a firm believer in the use of technology to communicate ideas. He first used cut-up film projections and audio tape, later using CD-ROMs and PCs—think Adobe Premiere, Macromedia Director, and QuickTime—and then the Internet. Joe and Nina then ran a digital storytelling institute of sorts, now called StoryCenter, where Joe remains executive director.

The workshop was a serious challenge. There were so many ideas I wanted to communicate as I crafted my brief video about the readers network. I planned to screen the story at stops along the forthcoming Company of Friends Roadshow, using it as a way to communicate the idea of the magazine, the idea of the network, why we were all there, and why someone should join. It was equal parts State of the Union and recruitment reel. And I only had a few minutes given the size of the resulting file and iMac computer processing power at the time.

The first thing I learned was that technology can—sometimes—help you more successfully communicate your idea. At the time, digital video and multimedia was still quite new, so the novelty aspect helped increase attention and interest.

I didn't just learn how to record and shoot audio and video, convert it to digital, and edit in Premiere. I learned how to boil an idea down to its bare essentials. Sometimes a small idea is more easily shared than a big idea. Sometimes you need to start small before offering the big picture. Focus on the key problem that's solved or the main opportunity offered, and build from there. In the case of the Company of Friends, the small idea was connection and collaboration with like-minded business people.

Another thing I learned was that it can sometimes be useful not to communicate your idea yourself. As the owner or initiator of the idea, you can enlist others to communicate your idea for you. Incorporating footage of readers meeting face to face in coffee shops and conference rooms, including member testimonials and stories, and featuring other real-life people as the primary speakers, the idea became more real.

People watching the video during the subsequent Roadshow events could see themselves in the idea, better understanding the personal and professional opportunity. My presence was just a voiceover narration in parts.

The bulk of the idea was communicated by members. That made it more powerful.

Section 4
Plan

"Let us make our future now, and let us make our dreams tomorrow's reality."

— MALALA YOUSAFZAI, ACTIVIST

So far, you have focused on preparing your idea—what you plan to communicate, and why—and yourself—as the communicator. Now you can turn your attention to the audience with which you plan to communicate.

This section—Plan—will focus on three steps that will help you focus specifically on your initial target audience and prepare to communicate with them specifically.

So far, your preparation has been general. As a communicator, you might find that you have multiple audiences. Those different audiences might have different interests and needs; this section will help you laser focus your attention on the specific interests and needs of a given target audience. It will also help you tailor your communication specifically for them.

Step 7
Take Aim

"Become genuinely interested in other people."

— DALE CARNEGIE, EDUCATOR

So far, you've focused on audience generally, and communication generally, though you've been thinking about your idea specifically. At this point in the process, you have looked at why you want to communicate an idea (Purpose), how you're going to package and present your idea (Package), and who you are personally as the communicator (Person). Now we can turn to the third part of Aristotle's simplified method of communication, the audience, or the receiver of your communication. Even though you've considered your audience throughout the book, you can now change your approach slightly and get much more specific. So doing, you'll not just define your primary target audience and refine your idea Package specifically for that audience. You'll also adjust your approach as a communicator to work more efficiently and effectively with that audience.

What Do You Want? (Reprise)

Return now to a previous section of the book, Step 2, "Land on an Ask," specifically the section "What Do You Want?" above.

Is your goal or desired response to your idea understanding, agreement, or action? If action is your desired outcome, what action do you want your audience to take after engaging with you? Refer to your notes in the "A Question for You" workbook portion and remind yourself what your goal for communicating this particular idea is. Reaffirm in your mind that it's important and interesting to you. Recommit to pursuing that desired outcome.

A Question for You

What do you want people to do as a response to your communication and idea? What is your most important Call to Action? What is the singular Ask you'll focus on?

_____

_____

_____

_____

_____

Has your goal changed at all over the course of the book? How so?

_____

_____

_____

_____

Do you need to adjust your goal at all as a result of those changes, if any?

_____

_____

_____

_____

_____

Whose Help Do You Need?

To accomplish your refined and confirmed goal above, whose help do you need? In marketing, professional marketers think about that in terms of target audience. Sometimes, marketers want to communicate the same thing to everyone, in the same way. It doesn't matter who they are, or what marketers say—in terms of being specific to them. However, to truly have impact as a communicator, you might want to identify which audience can be the most help to you.

Do you need to reach a specific kind of professional? Do you want to communicate with a decision maker in a particular department in an organization? Does it matter what kind of company you reach out to in order to do new business? Should you contact them at a specific time of the year, or the month, to best resonate with their attention and needs?

Who can help you the most? Does the organization or decision maker need a budget or an employee base of a certain size to truly benefit from your services? Are there any prerequisites for adopting your idea? Do they need any special kind of equipment or system in place to truly benefit from it? Are there any time-based requirements in terms of deadlines or seasonality?

In short, don't just pitch your idea to anyone or everyone, be *specific* in terms of who you reach out to and want to engage with. Be sure that they'll be high impact, open to your idea and approach, and responsive. Those are the qualities you should look for in your target audience.

A Question for You

Who or what is your target audience for communicating your idea?

_____

_____

_____

_____

_____

Why are they your target audience? Why do you need their help?

_____

_____

_____

_____

_____

If it's not a specific person, team, or organization, what are the qualities or characteristics of the kind of person, team, or organization you plan to target?

_____

_____

Are there any requirements or prerequisites that need to be addressed before your idea will work well for your target audience?

Target Your Audience

In addition to giving thought to whose help you need to bring your idea to reality—your target audience—give additional thought to how to best connect and interact with your idea or concept's general audience more broadly. In traditional marketing, your target audience might be the most important or highest priority portion of your overall audience, usually identified through an audience segmentation or other audience research. But there might be other audiences you'll still communicate with. They might be secondary audience segments. They might be other stakeholders who aren't necessarily the primary decision maker.

Let's expand on that idea a little more. An audience segmentation is a marketing research project that breaks a product, service, or company's potential audience into defined subsets that can be sized and targeted with marketing and advertising. An audience segmentation helps you not just identify the different subsets of your audience, but also size and prioritize them so you can work with the segment most open to your idea or messaging, the segment with the most money, the segment with the most influence, or the segment most likely to adopt a new technology—however you wish to prioritize selecting your target.

It's important to have your target audience or target segment in mind because you can then specifically target all of your marketing to them in order to have the most impact. If you market or communicate more broadly to your general audience, you won't communicate as specifically. You'll market to and communicate with everyone in the same way. When you target your audience and communicate specifically with your highest priority segment, you will consider your value propositions, positioning, messaging, even the media or channels you use to reach them—every aspect of marketing—specific to your target audience.

That will be useful when initially communicating your ideas, as well as in later communication and more general marketing communication. Even if you find yourself interacting with someone who's not necessarily representative of your highest priority audience segment, knowing more about your segments—perhaps through additional marketing research—will help you improve your communication with them.

A Question for You

What other audiences or audience segments might also be important?

How are they different from your highest priority target audience?

_____

_____

_____

_____

How and where can you best reach your target audience?

_____

_____

_____

_____

Know the Wants and Needs

Ideally, this step is taken when your idea, product, or service is initially being developed. Some of the most successful products and services are developed in direct response to customers' or potential customers' wants and needs. Even if your idea isn't necessarily the direct result of existing consumer—or community—needs, you can still benefit from learning more about what your audience wants and needs. (And how your idea connects and resonates with that.)

Return now to your notes in Step 2's segment on "What's in It for Me?" Those comments and remarks might be a useful foundation to return to this thinking. Similarly, in Step 5's segment titled "Make a

Difference," you gave additional thought to what problems your idea will help solve that other ideas might not as effectively address. But the best way to learn more about your target audience's wants and needs is to ask.

Sometimes, wants and needs will come up in discussion and conversation, but it can also be productive to ask explicitly. You'll be better able to speak to their needs (more on that below) if you know about them in advance. How you approach that will depend on the idea you're communicating, whether it's for a business, community group, or personal project, and other aspects. Sometimes it might be awkward to ask directly. Other times, you can ask by sending a survey or brief questionnaire to customers and potential customers.

A Question for You

Do you already know about your target audience's wants and needs? If so, what are they?

_____

_____

_____

_____

_____

If there are multiple wants and needs, how would you—or your audience—prioritize them? Which is most important?

_____

_____

_____

If you don't already know about their wants and needs, how can you best learn about them?

Focus on Problems and Tension

This is an important consideration. You will be most successful communicating an idea with your target audience if it directly resonates with them and helps them address a specific, existing problem or tension. That's really what you're going for when you consider your audience's wants and needs. (And when you prioritize them to identify the most important one.) If you can offer your idea as a solution to a problem or challenge that they are already facing—that already causes them pain, literal or figurative—they will be much more open to the idea, likely to consider it seriously, and prone to choose it among other competitive options.

Don't speak generally about other people's, team's, or organization's problems and challenges, though. Directly address your target audience's specific personal, professional, and organizational challenges once you've identified them—using the words they used to describe and detail them if you can—and offer your idea as a compelling solution to the problem. Offer your idea as the tool they can use to resolve whatever tension they might be experiencing. Help them become the hero they can be.

A Question for You

What is your target audience's primary pain point, problem, or tension?

_____

_____

_____

_____

_____

How does your idea directly address or relieve that problem or tension?

_____

_____

_____

_____

_____

Speak to Their Needs

By this time, everything you say and discuss with your target audience should respond to, be related to, and directly address their wants and needs. Your idea should clearly be positioned as a solution to problems or challenges they face, or a useful tool to help them accomplish their goals, mission, and vision for their own role, team or community, organization or company.

Interestingly, at this point, their wants and needs don't just help you better communicate the value and potential of your idea, product, or service. They can also help you develop or identify new ideas they might find useful.

By focusing on your highest priority audience, customer, or client—by learning more and more over time about what they want and need—and by continually seeking to help them solve problems, challenges, and issues that they face, you will become a true expert about and ally of or advocate for their business.

You might also discover that you can identify potential problems and challenges before they even occur, given your deepening knowledge of what your target audience does and how they do it.

Take note of those insights and ideas as you encounter them. Some might deserve additional development—to meet additional needs of your audience.

A Question for You

As you work with your target audience, do any additional wants and needs emerge as particularly interesting or important?

_____

_____

_____

_____

_____

Does communicating with your audience give you any new ideas? If so, what are they? How might you develop those new ideas, as well?

_____

_____

You have now completed Step 7, "Take Aim." You've returned to your personal motivation and goals as a communicator. You've identified whose help you need to accomplish those goals for yourself, your team, and your company—and you've targeted your primary audience, your most important audience segment, perhaps. You've detailed and described their wants and needs, addressed their challenges, problems, and tensions—and you've determined how your idea best meets their most important needs.

In Step 8, "Be Prepared," you'll pay attention to yourself as a communicator and become fully prepared to engage in a conversation and discussion with your target audience.

Step 8
Be Prepared

"If passion drives you, let reason hold the reins."

—BENJAMIN FRANKLIN, POLITICIAN

In Scouts BSA, this is the Scout Motto: "Be prepared." Once, someone asked Scouting's founder Robert Baden-Powell what Scouts should be prepared for. "Why, for any old thing," he replied. The same can be true in business—and in communications.

Particularly in terms of scenario planning, situational analysis, business development, competitive intelligence, sales, and marketing, it can be helpful to prepare for any eventuality. For any old thing. That way, you won't be surprised. You won't be caught at a loss. That way, you might even have a response or reaction that you've already identified, developed—and perhaps even rehearsed or roleplayed—so you can continue working toward your goals.

When communicating ideas, preparation has been important throughout the entire process so far—this book is almost entirely preparation! Now that you have identified who your target audience is—and what they want and need, what problems and tensions you can address—you can turn your preparation attention to actually engage with a fellow community member, prospect, business partner, or stakeholder in communication about your ideas. Consider this the preparation you would do at the end of your process to get ready to call on a prospect or someone you want to win over to your idea.

Prepare the Package

Go over your communication, message, hard copy takeaway, and idea Package one more time. Make sure it's the most recent version you've been working on. Make sure it's clearly worded, in good condition—regardless of whether it's a hard copy or soft copy, or something you prepare to say in person—and is as you'd like it to be.

One thing you can consider here is whether your material is too long or written too verbosely. Executive coach Maggie Craddock reminds us that people have short attention spans, and anything too long—written or presented—can make your audience lose interest. To address that, break your content and commentary up into smaller units so they're more digestible and people can process them before you move on to the next point. That approach can also make your communication more conversational.

Take time to review the different aspects and components of your message. Include some intertextual references and remarks if you're able to.

Once you're satisfied that your message, communication, or hard copy is as it should be, you can turn your attention to a few specific aspects of what you plan to communicate.

A Question for You

Is your ideas Package ready to go? Are there any last minute refinements, improvements, or changes you need to make?

_____

_____

_____

Know the Value of Your Idea

It's important that you make a compelling case to your colleague or prospect, your audience, that your idea or offer has adequate value and is worth consideration. So take another moment now to reconsider and reevaluate the value of your offer.

Think about value in two ways. First of all, think about the value propositions you've identified for your idea in Step 2, "Land on an Ask," and Step 4, "Seek the Shine," above. What does your idea offer them? What will it do for them?

Also think about value in terms of cost. For your idea to be compelling, the value or upside brought by the idea will need to be greater than any cost or downside to implementing the idea. Even if that value and cost isn't communicated explicitly, be sure that you can accurately suggest that the idea has more merit than it has detriment.

Another way to consider the value of your idea is in light of the challenges, problems, and tensions it addresses. Return to Step 7 above, "Take Aim," and calculate or estimate any possible costs associated with those tensions.

I find it necessary here to warn you against the idea of the hyperbolic "Million Dollar Idea." Chances are that most of your ideas won't be worth a million dollars. So when calculating value, try to be as realistic as possible. How dare I say your idea isn't worth a million dollars? Think about it. What you consider to be the most important problem might not be your audience's most important problem. If no one else is currently doing what you'd like to do, a total lack of competition could indicate that it's not actually a good idea. And even if you succeed at communicating your idea well, now the proof is in the pudding: Can you *act* on your idea? As we see with competitors such as Fisker Inc. and Tesla Inc., ideas might be similar, but implementation can vary.

Take time now to review your idea's value propositions and benefits to address existing tensions, as well as the value and potential costs of implementing the idea—so you can clearly make the case that your idea will bring more benefits than liabilities.

A Question for You

Even if estimating, what is the possible value of implementing your idea?

_____

_____

_____

_____

_____

Likewise, what are the possible costs of implementing your idea?

_____

_____

_____

_____

_____

Which is greater, the value or the cost?

_____

_____

_____

Ask the Questions They'll Ask

Fully in the spirit of "Be prepared," think ahead to what questions your target audience might ask about your idea. Write them down. Develop answers and responses to those questions. It might also be useful to come up with additional, other questions. There are two useful exercises to undertake. One, come up with five different versions of each question you've already written down. Those can be similar to the original questions, or they can be slightly different. They can also be new, different questions entirely. Undertaking this exercise will help you develop a better sense of what a person might ask, and how. Even if the questions are similar, considering different ways that they can be asked will help you better respond in real life.

You might also find that the slightly different wordings of the questions lead to or suggest new and other questions entirely. Address those questions, as well—and consider whether you can identify any general patterns in the way that new questions develop. Does that tendency to change suggest any additional questions or issues?

Secondly, undergo an exercise called the Question Behind the Question. For each question you initially listed as a possible question someone might ask, write another question—the question that they might actually asking but haven't asked yet, or the question behind the question. Do that five times for each question, each time building on the new, as yet unasked question. (This is not just five new questions inspired by the original question. In this exercise, each subsequent new question inspires a new, unasked question.)

It can also be helpful to be as specific and detailed as you can be in the questions you develop. Deborah Shames, co-founder of business presentation and communication training company Eloqui, says that general, open-ended questions can be more challenging or vague to answer. Specific, more pointed or directed questions might be more productive and useful.

Regardless of the approach you use, you might find it helpful and productive to rank order and prioritize the new questions you've developed. Which questions are most important? Which are most challenging?

A Question for You

What questions do you expect your target audience to ask?

_____

_____

_____

_____

_____

What questions do you think they'll have but not necessarily ask?

_____

_____

_____

_____

_____

Which questions do you think are the most important or challenging?

_____

_____

_____

Handle Objections

Similar to the previous section, in addition to coming up with what questions your target audience might ask you before they ask, we can also take a cue from the world of sales, and give thought to what objections your audience might have to your idea. You should already have some ideas for possible objections. Start by listing those—reasons your audience might offer for why your idea is a bad idea, won't work, costs too much, or otherwise poses a challenge. That could even encompass situations in which the perceived cost of your idea outweighs the perceived value from above. Then spend some more time, perhaps 10-15 minutes, writing down other objections or problems with your idea—reasons it won't work or someone shouldn't act on it.

Once you've created that list of objections, draft your responses and counterarguments to those objections. Refute them with value propositions, characteristics, or other aspects of your idea. Offer explanations for why an objection or concern is unfounded. Document experiences or examples from other people you've encountered or experienced to allay concern about a given aspect of your idea.

Be prepared to address objections your audience might have as you communicate your idea. Be prepared to handle and manage problems, challenges, and issues they identify. That is a common sales technique, and it's useful when communicating more generally, as well.

A Question for You

What objections might your audience raise to your idea?

What might you say or do to overcome those objections?

Respond Immediately

The goal of this section is to enable and prepare you to respond to your audience while you're communicating with them with the additional information, details, and answers they might need to make an informed decision. You want to be able to adequately address, handle, and manage any problems, challenges, or objections your audience might offer in response to your idea while you're communicating with them.

You want to be prepared to answer your audience's questions and address their concerns immediately. Don't rush your response. Don't respond defensively. Share the additional information, context, and point of view at an appropriate pace. But don't make them wait. And don't leave.

If you leave your audience without addressing their questions and concerns—if you have to "get back to them"—the odds of your idea landing solidly and successfully diminish substantially. Their concerns might grow in importance in the interim, and their interest—though initially high—might diminish. In addition, your audience might interpret your inability to respond immediately as being unprepared generally—or not being able to address their concerns more broadly.

So it's best to adequately prepare, again, "for any old thing," so you can keep your communication to this moment in time, taking the opportunity to respond to your audience's questions and objections—and giving them the chance to make a decision or act on it now. Don't make them wait until later because you're not fully prepared or ready as the communicator. Take the opportunity to communicate when it's offered.

A Question for You

Do you feel adequately prepared to address questions and objections when they arise?

_____

_____

_____

_____

_____

If you don't feel adequately prepared yet, what do you need to do in order to prepare fully?

_____

_____

_____

_____

_____

Practice Makes Perfect

To get good at doing something, to become adept and expert, you have to practice.

We've all heard the joke: "How do you get to Carnegie Hall?" "Practice."

Over the years, that punchline has been credited to Jascha Heifetz, Artur Rubinstein, an anonymous musician or taxi driver, even to a beatnik. But no one really knows where the joke came from. It might have originated in vaudeville or emerged out of Borscht Belt comedy in the Catskills. But the joke stands, and has stood for decades: "How do you get to Carnegie Hall?"

"Practice."

Long-time marketing consultant and copywriter Dan Kennedy once told me a story about the actor Yul Brynner. Even though Brynner performed *The King & I* many, many times on Broadway, he still continued to rehearse his facial expressions, hand gestures, and lines every single day. Brynner did so before each performance, for the run of the show. Every single day.

Both vignettes suggest to me that you can never assume that you've "got this," or that you'll be able to do what you want to do well when you're called to do so. Instead, do what Brynner did:

Practice.

Write out a script detailing word for word what you'd like to say in any given situation. Practice reciting the script until it's natural and conversational. Record yourself and listen to it to learn how to improve your content and delivery. Roleplay it with or practice in front of members of your family, friends, teammates, and others to seek their feedback and input.

Consider practicing responding to your audience's expected questions and objections, as well. Practice—just like you might prepare—for any old thing.

However, Cameron Kiosoglous, program director at Drexler University's Sport Coaching Leadership Program, would remind you that too much practice without an explicit purpose can lead to stagnation and a weakening of your communication muscles. Also the U.S. Rowing National Team's coach, Kiosoglous recommends practicing to perform, not just practicing to practice. You need to refine your approach to the technical aspects of your communication, but you also need to experiment and explore within that. Practice can help you find that freedom if you don't let yourself get stale.

If you've never practiced how you're going to communicate with an audience before, start now. Practice to perform. And if you already practice to this extent, do so even more frequently. Because only practice makes perfect.

A Question for You

Do you make it a habit to practice or rehearse what you want to communicate?

_____

_____

_____

_____

_____

Do you practice or roleplay with family, friends, teammates, or colleagues?

_____

_____

_____

_____

_____

Do you practice responding to questions or handling objections, too?

You have now completed Step 8, "Be Prepared," which focused on being as prepared to communicate as you can possibly be—being prepared "for any old thing." That step helped you finalize preparing your idea Package for the target audience, calculating and considering the value of your idea, planning for any questions or objections that might arise, preparing to respond to such questions and objections immediately rather than make your audience wait, and practicing your communication for delivery.

In the next step, you'll prepare yourself personally, as a Person, to communicate.

Step 9
Brace Yourself

"Confidence is a lot of this game or any game. If you don't think you can, you won't."

— JERRY WEST, ATHLETE

If Step 8, "Be Prepared," is about preparation, consider this step the things you might do in the Green Room before giving a talk at a conference, in the restroom at the mirror before going into an important board meeting or sales pitch, or at your desk or on the couch before you make that next cold call.

Whether you do vocal warmups like performance coach and author Brendon Burchard, jumping jacks or light calisthenics, or say the word "great" five time to enhance your smile and improve the tone of your voice, there are actions you can undertake to "get in the zone."

This step will give you tactics and tips that will help you increase your energy, improve your presence, and make yourself a more engaging, interesting, and successful communicator.

Dress for Success

Do not just wear what you want to wear. Wear what the person who's about to communicate what you want to communicate would wear.

Wear what you expect your audience to wear. Wear what your audience expects *you* to wear. Or, dress just a little better—or worse—than they might, so you're different, but not too different. You want to play the role they expect you to play, and to play the role of a successful, persuasive, compelling communicator.

You also want to play a role that is in service of your idea. That can be a balancing act. You want to meet the needs and expectations of your audience, be true to yourself so you're comfortable and accurately representing yourself, and reflect the power and potential of your idea so there's no cognitive dissonance between you and your idea.

Do not let your clothing undermine your message, challenge your credibility, or otherwise raise questions or concerns in the mind of your audience. You want your outfit and presence to be the frosting on the cake and the bow on the present, not kick the tires out from under you.

Do not let the way you dress for the speaking engagement, meeting, or workshop suggest a lack of preparation for or commitment to your interaction with your audience.

A Question for You

What do you normally wear for work? What accessories or tools do you usually use for work?

_____

_____

_____

_____

_____

How will your audience be dressed and equipped for your time together?

_____

_____

_____

_____

_____

If your idea were a person, how would your idea dress and outfit itself?

_____

_____

_____

_____

_____

Increase the Energy

To be most effective as a communicator, you will want to exhibit and maintain a high level of energy, but not to the extent that you seem frantic, over the top, or otherwise off-putting. Be sure that you've had a good night's sleep before you need to communicate something important, and consider doing some light exercise or calisthenics before the conversation or presentation. (Maybe even have a cup of coffee, tea, or an energy drink if that's your speed!) Some communicators like to do jumping jacks just before they go in to meet with their audience.

You might also experience, however, that you tend to get keyed up, agitated, or nervous before communicating something important. If that is instead the case, you will want to calm down and focus instead of getting your blood flowing. Take a series of deep breaths. Sit still and meditate on something calming, while concentrating your breath. Or engage in other centering exercises to bring your pulse under control and to relax a little before you meet with your audience.

Kathleen Harshberger, author of *Etiquette Still Matters*, says that friendly eye contact is key to good communication. But remember that too intense eye contact can be off putting. Look at the space between the eyebrows, and it'll seem like you're looking at them, but not too intensely or aggressively. Try not to look away or down, though. Your audience might interpret that as dishonesty or hiding something.

Also, concentrate on your posture. Regardless of whether you are sitting or standing, do so straight—don't let a slouch or slumped shoulders suggest a lack of confidence or competence. And remain aware of your audience's body language as you spend time with them. Remain open to them, facing them, and fully focused and engaged with them. Pay attention to gestures, as well.

In Step 6, "Power Up," we considered how you can read your audience's body language and posture as a communications signal. Remember that *your* body language and posture, your energy, is communicating to your audience, as well.

A Question for You

Do you generally need to increase your energy before communicating with an audience? Or do you need to calm down and relax instead?

_____

_____

_____

_____

_____

What energy-increasing or -centering activities tend to work best for you? What are your go-to practices that you can depend on?

_____

_____

_____

_____

_____

In terms of body language, what do you need to concentrate on most: your speech diction, pace, and patterns; your gestures and how you hold your hands; or other aspects of your movement and posture?

_____

_____

_____

_____

_____

Go Where They Are

As the communicator, while you might be able to control the frame and context of your discussion and communication, if there is something that you *want* from your audience—that you will ask them for (see Step 2, "Land on an Ask," above)—you are the supplicant, in a way.

So go to them. Don't make them come to you.

Make yourself available. Make yourself convenient. Make your schedule open, flexible, and available to them, and meet when it's best for them—as well as where they'd like to meet. In some cases, that might not even be in person. For example, Anjee Solanki, national director of retail services for commercial real estate and investment management company Colliers International, realized that online resources such as podcasts and webinars can sometimes be useful, even necessary. Your preference might be to communicate in person, but if you can't, consider a video conference, a web event or webinar, a podcast, or another online solution.

You don't have to control where communication is located or worry about "home court advantage." You can only control what you can control: yourself, your communication, and how you respond to their reactions.

You can do that anywhere, in many ways. So go and be wherever they want to meet with you—how they want to meet with you—when you communicate, and be there fully.

A Question for You

Are you able to make yourself fully available to your audience?

_____

_____

_____

_____

If your communications plan includes any materials or audio-visual equipment or other technological needs, are you able to prepare them for transportation to your audience? Is there anything you need them to prepare on site in addition to whatever you bring?

_____

_____

_____

_____

Right Time, Right Place

Sometimes, though, your communication might not be formally scheduled in advance of an opportunity that arises off the cuff and unexpectedly. In those cases, you will need to decide if the chance encounter or crossing of paths is the right time and place for you to bring up the topic of interest or import. Sometimes it is, but sometimes it might not be.

You will need to decide whether the time and place is appropriate to broach the topic. If it is, are you prepared to take advantage of the opportunity? If you aren't prepared—if it's not the right place or time—is now the time to suggest *scheduling* a time? Or do you leave that for another time?

How do you know if it's the right place or time? Consider the opportunity from your point of view, as well as from the audience's. Are you ready? Are you comfortable, confident, and fully prepared to do the best you can possibly do right now? Do you have what you need with you to fully make your case? If you don't take this opportunity, will you miss out on a window of opportunity? Or can you reasonably loop back again sometime soon, with no opportunity lost?

And from their point of view, are they harried, distracted, in a rush, or otherwise unable to fully concentrate on interacting with you? Would it be awkward or rude for you to bring up your topic of interest given the current setting? For example, it might not be appropriate for you to make a business proposal at a family gathering. At other times, it might be. Regardless, you don't necessarily need to jump on the opportunity, if it's a less opportune time for the audience to be fully receptive to your communication.

Consider your preparedness, as well as your audience's. And remember that they are the more important party in the situation.

A Question for You

Are you prepared such that if a chance opportunity arises you can take advantage of it?

_____

_____

_____

_____

_____

Is this a situation that should be more formally scheduled and planned for?

_____

_____

_____

_____

_____

Limit Distractions

In a professional speaking, meeting, or more formal business situation, this mostly takes care of itself. You'll still want to do a quick spot check to address any immediate biological needs before you start the discussion.

Personally, I usually check on three things. Do I have to go to the bathroom? Am I thirsty or do I need a drink of water, or do I want water near at hand? And am I too warm or too cold? Am I wearing appropriate layers so I can be flexible and change as needed? Usually, if I can take care of those three needs just before starting a conversation or presentation, the rest can fall into place on its own. But there's nothing worse than being distracted by having to urinate while you're trying to communicate something important. Seriously.

There are other distractions you'll want to consider, too. Are you in a place with too much nearby ambient noise or competing conversations? Are you in a high traffic area with movement and other visual distractions? Does the person you plan to communicate with have another meeting or appointment too soon—will you have adequate time to consider, address, and discuss the topic at hand?

Do you have adequate privacy? If your communication involves anything sensitive or proprietary, are you in an appropriate setting for such a discussion or presentation? Will your audience be self-conscious about passersby, or people being able to see any materials, or perhaps overhear details from your conversation?

And lastly, try to limit your media, social media, or email and mobile phone use just before you go into a communication situation. You don't need to be distracted by bad news in terms of current events and world affairs. You don't need to be thinking about a situation at work that just popped up—instead of your communication. You don't need to try to remember any new action items or to-do's. And only the biggest emergencies at home would pull you out of a meeting or discussion, so don't burden yourself with potential distractions or worries until afterward, when you're on your own again. Focus on where you are, who you're with, and what you want to say or talk about.

A Question for You

Will you be able to take water with you? Adequate layered clothing?

_____

_____

_____

Based on where your communication will occur, are there any distractions or eventualities you should plan for? How can you best address
any challenges that arise?

_____

_____

_____

_____

_____

Ready the Target

Similar to how you just checked in with yourself to be sure that you
weren't uncomfortable or otherwise distracted or preoccupied, it's
important that you also check in with your audience. You might not
be able to as clearly or as explicitly, but do what you can to make sure
that they have the time, space, attention, and comfort necessary to
fully engage with you.

The degree to which you do that will depend on the seriousness or
import of the topic or opportunity, as well as the audience's receptivity
and openness to the idea. (Consider for a moment the proverbial,
"You'll want to sit down for this," before delivering bad news, for
example.) Sometimes the most you can do is confirm that the time is
still a good time, and that you have their full attention.

If anything else comes up while you're communicating, you can
always address them like you would objections or questions, which

we've explored above in Step 8, "Be Prepared." But do so with a spirit of patience, generosity, and empathy.

A Question for You

What might your audience need on site while you communicate? Can you perhaps prepare to help meet any needs that might arise for them?

_____

_____

_____

_____

_____

You have now completed Step 9, "Brace Yourself," in which you decided what to wear for your communications situation, maintained a high level of energy, approached your audience at the right place and right time, limited distractions that could impede your communication, and prepared your audience as best you could.

In the next step, you'll actually communicate your idea, making your pitch—and telling a story.

Communicating My Ideas Case Study #4: National Day of Prayer

In 2017, inspired by 24-7 Prayer, the International House of Prayer, the National Day of Prayer, and the International Day of Prayer, I was interested in organizing a 24-hour prayer vigil in my home town. Members of local churches, temples, and other religious organizations would participate in the event in the spring of 2018. The event was intended to encourage daily prayer and to help recognize the National Day of Prayer with a crowd-sourced and distributed prayer vigil that combined personal and group prayer, worship, and music. It would encourage prayer, foster ties between area faith communities, bridge generations, and perhaps even plant the seed of establishing a 24-7 Prayer Room locally.

I planned to send letters of introduction to more than 40 faith community leaders of local churches and other potential sites, hoping to identify local site coordinators. Those people would then work with me to mobilize parishioners and others affiliated with the church, temple, or site. The target audience for participants included area church members and youth group members; Scouts BSA and Girl Scout units; Alcoholics Anonymous and other 12-step meetings affiliated with churches; university and college student groups; fraternal organizations and service clubs such as the Kiwanis and Masons; and senior centers, and elderly and care homes.

People would sign up for time slots. Across all the sites, we'd have people praying non-stop for 24 hours, at the sites and in their homes. If interest were sufficient, there'd be spiritual readings, talks, guided meditations, musical performances, and other special events scheduled to punctuate the personal and group prayer.

I developed a project brief, a task list for site coordinators, a sign-up sheet coordinators could use, and a master schedule. I mailed the letters to the more than 40 faith community leaders. And in the end, only one faith community expressed interest—my own home church—and even there, no one signed up for a time slot.

The idea remains a good idea, in fact, a big, beautiful idea—one I intend to return to—but my communication of it in 2017-2018 soundly flopped. And flopped hard. But I learned several things, which I'll draw on when I return to the idea in the future.

First of all, multiple audiences require increased attention, energy, and focus. Not only was I hoping to work with more than 40 different faith communities, they came from different faiths and required slightly different communication. Similarly, I had a dual audience when considering the faith community leader, the site coordinator, and the parishioners or community members. Each had different communication needs, and I didn't do an adequate job targeting the most important audience first: the community leader. (That could be seen as similar to business-to-business communications. You have your audience at the business, and then you have *their* audience. You need to keep both in mind.)

I also learned that warm contacts are better than cold contacts. The one church that responded in any way was my home church. (Go figure!) Our existing relationship, friendship, and time together at least got me the attention of the community leader and a site coordinator. But relying on them to target the next audience—the participants—fell short.

That taught me two things. You cannot rely on someone else to communicate your idea for you unless they've fully bought into it and fully prepared to communicate it on your behalf. You might very well be the most informed, invested, and impassioned person supporting your idea. That energy goes really far. Also, you have to go to your audience, not wait for them to come to you. Not once did I meet in person with a community leader, church committee, or speak in front of a congregation. I didn't even call them on the telephone. I relied on others—also cold contacts—to do my communication work for me. Without strong advocates and allies, the idea sat on folks' desks in an envelope rather than coming to life around town. Relationships matter, and without them, it's much more challenging to communicate a new idea.

In the end, I failed to successfully communicate the idea, and to bring it to life. I still think it's a good idea, and I plan to return to it differently and more intently in the future. I will focus much less on the end of the process—the sign-up sheets and coordinator task lists—and more on the Plan to communicate my idea.

That's where I fell short.

Section 5
Pitch

"If you don't create your reality, your reality will create you."
— LIZZIE WEST, MUSICIAN

You have almost reached the end of the process you began at the start of this book—approaching the point where many books and courses on communicating ideas begin. Finally, you are about to communicate, not "merely" prepare to communicate. (Those air quotes are laden with sarcasm.) You've spent most of your time on the conditioning and the wind up that we mentioned at the beginning of the book. Now you're approaching the release, the Pitch.

Hopefully, it's clear now how much preparation an experienced communicator can do before they actually jump right into their story, pitch, or call to action. Hopefully, it's also clear to you how much more prepared, confident, and competent preparation can help you become as a communicator of ideas.

While many business leaders and professionals might consider the Pitch itself the most challenging part of the process—the most high stakes—I have found that if I prepare adequately, that is actually the easy part. Having gone through the other stages of the process, you have focused on your Purpose, idea Package, Person as a communicator, and communications Plan. Having taken the other nine steps you've already covered and explored, the Pitch might even come as second nature and be somewhat comfortable and familiar. That has been our goal.

Some of the best communicators in the world seem extremely relaxed, natural, and comfortable—even during high-stress situations, business proposals that can make or break their business, and main stage conference and convention speeches in front of thousands of people.

In fact, preparing to that extent will help make you a more comfortable and natural communicator, too. That preparation frees you up to focus more on your message and audience rather than the logistics or mechanics of delivery. You will be much better able to pay attention, react, and respond to your audience.

After all, you are communicating because there is something you want to accomplish. There is something you want your audience to do as a result of your communication. That's where you are now—about to make your Pitch.

Step 10
Tell a Story

"A problem well stated is a problem half solved."

— CHARLES KETTERING, INVENTOR

The most comfortable and natural way for human beings to communicate is through stories. Stories have been how humans have communicated from time immemorial. When communicating ideas, there are several different kinds of stories you can tell.

Most of the stories ever told fall under one of the following seven kinds of stories. They are the Underdog story (or Conquering the Monster), the Quest, the Journey and Return, Rags to Riches, Comedy (or the Clarity Tale), Tragedy (or the Cautionary Tale), and Rebirth.

When reading a book, watching TV, watching a movie, or listening to a TED Talk—even when in conversation with a friend or colleague—see if you can detect or determine what kind of story they are telling. It will be rare indeed for a story not to fit into one of those seven categories.

In fact, consider those seven story types and decide which story type—or types—might best suit how you'll approach telling your story to and communicating your idea to your audience. You can apply the types to a story you tell about yourself or your organization, about your audience, as well as about how your idea might affect your audience.

Your audience's story—or a more personal story—can also matter. Sharon Patterson, an executive at talent development firm Lee Hecht Harrison, encourages leaders to also seek and share stories about personal interests such as hobbies or favored activities. Telling stories about who you are, as well as what you do, doesn't just make you more accessible, it can form stronger bonds with your audience, perhaps increasing trust.

Remain flexible and open-minded as you consider how to best apply story to communicating your idea. The story you choose might depend on your idea, your audience, their needs, and other aspects specific to your situation—and your self.

The Elements of a Story

Regardless of what kind of story you plan to tell—or prepare to be able to tell—all stories will have the same common elements. Give thought to each element as they apply to your Pitch and consider them in the context of the story you'd like to tell and the idea you'd like to communicate.

The elements of a story include character, setting, plot, conflict, and theme. We'll address conflict directly below, considering it in the context of a tension, which we've touched on already above in Step 7, "Take Aim." That conflict or tension might even be the most important part of your story and the idea you're communicating. Regardless, spend some time identifying ways to address and consider the other elements of your story as you communicate with your audience.

A Question for You

Who are the characters in the story you might tell about your idea? If you are a character, who are you? If your audience is a character, who are they?

_____

_____

_____

_____

What is the setting? Where does the drama of your audience's conflict—and your idea—unfold?

_____

_____

_____

_____

What's going on? What's happening?

_____

_____

_____

_____

What is the primary conflict or tension in the story of your idea?

_____

_____

_____

_____

_____

What theme comes into play? If you could sum up your idea or its impact in one word, what is that word? If you could sum up the challenge facing your audience — or the problem your idea solves — in one word, what is that word?

_____

_____

_____

_____

_____

The Three-Act Structure

Stories also have a somewhat consistent structure, at least in narrative fiction and film, even in stage dramas such as plays. The three common parts of a story include three acts: the Setup, the Confrontation, and the Resolution.

Most of the elements explored above will come into play during the Setup, but the Confrontation is particularly important. Confrontation is when your audience's conflict comes into play most explicitly and openly. We'll explore that further — as tension — below.

The Confrontation is what requires your idea to come into play. The confrontation is what makes your idea necessary, and the resulting conflict—or tension—is relieved by your idea. Your idea solves the problem, the conflict.

A Question for You

Briefly describe your story's Setup. This only needs to be a rough draft or outline.

_____

_____

_____

_____

_____

Briefly describe your story's Confrontation. This also only needs to be a rough draft or outline.

_____

_____

_____

_____

_____

What primary problem, conflict, or tension comes into play during the Confrontation?

_____

Briefly describe your story's Resolution. This, too, only needs to be a rough draft or outline.

Tell Your Story

One of the challenging aspects of this particular kind of story, a story in service of communicating your idea, is that you or your organization are a character in it. But your role, while important, is not the most important role. Regardless, it is important that you include yourself, your organization, and your idea in the story you tell.

Take a moment and return to the section on "What's In It For Me?" above in Step 2, "Land on an Ask." Reviewing your notes there might help inform who you are as a character, as well as your *implicit* story in this situation.

Your implicit story—including your tension and your goals—might not be told as part of the telling, however, even if they remain ever in the background. Regardless, returning to those interests will help clarify your motivations as a character in the story.

A Question for You

Who are you as a character in the story?

_____

_____

_____

_____

_____

What is your character's story?

_____

_____

_____

_____

What role do you play as a character?

_____

_____

_____

_____

_____

Tell Your Audience's Story

The story you will tell to your audience, however, is a different, *explicit* story. It is a story about your audience, the problems that they face—conflict, confrontation, tension—and how your idea addresses that conflict. That is a more important story than *your* personal or professional story, because it focuses on the wants and needs, the problems and challenges, the situation faced by your audience. That's the story they care most about.

Larry Schmitt, managing partner at the Inovo Group, a consulting firm, suggests that this story can take one of two forms. Your story can either indicate your audience's desire or need that your idea addresses, or it can paint the picture of a future your audience would like to help create. In some situations, posing the story as a challenge or problem to solve might be too negative for the audience. If that seems likely, turn instead to a story that focuses more on creating a new future together.

It might be useful to return to the "What's In It for Me?" and "Know the Wants and Needs" sections in Step 2, "Land on an Ask," and Step 7, "Take Aim," above to consider several ways your idea might come into play and relieve their tension, addressing their problems directly.

Remember the three acts of a story: setup, confrontation, and resolution. I consider your idea addressing the problems and challenges of your audience during the confrontation as the volleyball bump, set, and spike of communicating ideas.

A Question for You

Who is your audience as a character (or characters) in the story?

What is their character's story?

_____

_____

_____

_____

_____

What role do they play as a character?

_____

_____

_____

_____

Address the Tension

This section addresses what is arguably the most important part of the story you tell when communicating your idea. The tension addressed during the Confrontation is the primary problem, challenge, conflict, struggle, bother, hassle, or other cause for confrontation for your audience as a character. Consider this their bottom, their pit—their deep, dark valley of the soul.

The tension is the primary problem your audience faces. In some cases, they might want to accomplish something, but face a barrier or blockage. In other cases, they might have a desire or a goal, but not have the resources or tools—or skills—to accomplish it.

Return to the section on "Know the Wants and Needs" above in Step 7, "Take Aim," for some ideas of what the tension might be in this specific situation and story. Sometimes, there might be more than one tension. Take some time to prioritize them, in terms of likelihood, as well as in terms of importance or impact.

Your idea can directly address that tension. That solution—your idea as hero—might be the most important part of the story.

You can explore that next.

A Question for You

What is the primary tension faced by your audience as a character?

_____

_____

_____

_____

The Idea as Hero

In the story you tell when communicating your idea, you or your organization are a character as the bearer or carrier of the idea, and your audience is a character as the person or party facing a conflict, confrontation, or tension. Your idea can also be seen as a character of sorts.

In a way, your idea is the good knight that rides in to lance and defeat the evil knight. Your idea is the brave hero freeing the bound victim held hostage by the hurtful antagonist. Your idea arrives just in the nick of time to defuse the dynamite at the entrance to the mine.

Your idea is what addresses the characters' conflict and confrontation, addressing and relieving the resulting tension. Your idea has come to save the day, just like Mighty Mouse.

Somewhat.

As you'll explore in the next step, your idea is not in fact the hero— but helps your audience become the hero. You'll spend more time exploring that soon.

A Question for You

Who is your idea as a character? How is your idea the hero?

_____

_____

_____

_____

_____

How does your idea address and relieve the tension?

_____

_____

_____

_____

You have just finished Step 10, "Tell a Story," in which you explored the elements of a story, the three-act structure to storytelling, how you and your audience's stories connect, the tension your idea addresses, and how your idea can play the role of the hero.

In the next step, you'll consider additional possible aspects and elements of your story that will improve and increase the impact of your communication.

Step 11
Push the Buttons

"If you want to be a great company, think about what social problems you could solve."

— JACK MA, BUSINESS PERSON

In the previous step, Step 10, "Tell a Story," you learned about how you can structure your communication like a story, incorporating the elements, structure, and other aspects of stories—and making the story personal, for you as well as for your audience. You also considered how you can position and offer your idea as the solution—the hero—to help overcome whatever conflict, confrontation, or tension your audience might face in their personal and professional lives.

There are additional things you can do while you're in the midst of communicating. I call the ideas in this step "Push the Buttons" because you're not just communicating at this point, you're communicating with some urgency.

You're communicating with intent and purpose to accomplish your goals, as well as those of your audience.

Speak Their Language

We addressed this above in Step 3, "Keep It Simple," but the focus is slightly different now. Not only do you generally need to communicate your idea in everyday language that the average person will understand, but now that you've better identified your audience and are communicating with them, you can be a little more specific—and a little less general—in the words you choose to use.

To some extent, if your audience is using, would likely use, or is certain to understand specific professional language, slang, lingo, or jargon, you can free yourself up a little to use it yourself. Use language that will speak directly to your audience, in a way that they're used to be spoken to, and in a way that will resonate with them directly given the setting you're in. Also, use language that will position you as an authority, expert, or trusted partner in that context.

At the same time, you can also pay attention to the words, phrases, and language that your audience is using while discussing the challenge, opportunity, or idea with you—and use similar words yourself. That can help establish stronger rapport with the audience, and help you better communicate using their own words.

A Question for You

Does your audience generally use any jargon, lingo, or slang?

What words or phrases does your audience otherwise use with some frequency that you can use to better communicate with them?

Poke the Pain

While communicating with your audience, you want to keep the conflict, confrontation, and tension firmly in mind—and front and center as you communicate.

In some ways, that approach can come close to feeling like you're poking a wound, peeling a scab, or otherwise irritating a sore spot for your audience. The important thing is to keep the problem firmly in mind, as the primary problem to solve or challenge to overcome. Their primary motivation for seeking new ideas and solutions could perhaps become the primary driver for them to adopt yours.

You can focus on how the problem or pain point is negatively affecting them by offering examples you've already encountered or validated. You can also ask your audience what the situation is keeping them from accomplishing. Additionally, you can ask what extra efforts and steps they have to make and take to work around the barrier. Focus on how the problem—the confrontation, the tension—makes their personal or professional life more difficult.

At some point, you want to transition from focusing on the negative—what are they being kept from doing, what pain are they experiencing—to focusing on the positive. If things were different, what might they be able to do? If they overcame the problem or challenge, how would they feel? If they no longer had to deal with the issue, what would they have more time, energy, and attention to do instead? What do they imagine being able to do?

Shift from focusing on the pain of the problem to the pleasure of overcoming the challenge—the resulting relief and freedom. That will help prepare both of you to consider solutions, and what adopting solutions might mean in their situation.

A Question for You

What primary pain does your audience experience?

_____

_____

_____

_____

_____

How does that pain affect your audience?

_____

_____

_____

_____

How does your idea serve as the solution to that problem?

_____

_____

_____

Solve Problems

Your intent and desire is to solve your audience's specific problems, overcome their challenges, and otherwise free them up to do other, perhaps more important, more effective things to succeed in work and life. While communicating with your audience, regardless of the setting, you can focus on identifying problems, challenges, and barriers to success. Consider how they might overcome those in order to better and more easily and effectively succeed and proceed. Position your idea as the ideal solution, right here, right now.

Of course, the degree to which you focus on and emphasize that depends on the situation, problems faced, and idea offered. Suggesting a movie for friends to see next weekend might not be as high stakes as offering your coaching services to an executive leading a high-turnover sales team. As the communicator, you can tone down or ratchet up the problem-solved aspect as much as is appropriate given the situation.

Regardless, focus on solving your audience's problems, overcoming their challenges, and otherwise being of service to them.

A Question for You

How will your idea solve your audience's problem?

How important is it that you concentrate on problem solving in your specific situation?

_____

_____

_____

_____

Offer Your Audience a Tool

One way you can best be of service to your audience to overcome problems and challenges is to offer them a clear solution. Communicate your idea as a tool your audience can use to accomplish their goals. In Step 10, "Tell a Story," we suggested that your idea can play the role of a hero that can overcome the audience's challenge.

Here, we're adjusting that concept slightly. Your idea is not the hero (more on that below). But your idea is a tool that your *audience* can use to overcome their challenge or problem.

Your idea is the solution. Your idea is their weapon—and perhaps even armor. Your idea is a tool, the ideal tool for them to use.

A Question for You

How will implementing your idea solve your audience's problem?

_____

_____

_____

How can you help them implement the idea?

_____

_____

_____

_____

_____

Be Convenient

In Step 4, "Seek the Shine," we looked at the value and cost offered by a given solution. Not only are you offering your idea as a tool your audience can use to solve their problem and overcome their challenges, your idea isn't hard to use.

Your idea is right here, offered by you. It is easy to understand, implement, and otherwise leverage.

In fact, if you've adequately prepared to communicate your idea, you already have your ask in mind. What can your audience do immediately to take advantage of your idea and resolve the conflict, confrontation, and tension that they face?

Make it easy and convenient for your audience to not just implement your idea, but to do so right here, right now.

A Question for You

How can they immediately take advantage of the idea?

_____

_____

_____

_____

_____

What next steps does your audience need to take to adopt your idea?

_____

_____

_____

_____

How soon can your audience get started?

_____

_____

_____

_____

Make Your Audience the Hero

Now is when you slightly refine the concept of idea as hero, from above. Your idea isn't the hero—your audience is.

Your audience becomes the hero by picking up on and adopting the idea you propose and offer. Implementing your idea can help your audience overcome whatever conflict, confrontation, or tension they're currently facing in their personal and professional life.

By accepting your help—and the merits and effects of your idea— your audience becomes the problem solver, the overcomer, the barrier breaker for their family, team, company, organization, or community. You are helping them succeed by offering your idea as a solution that's easy to adopt and implement.

Return briefly to "What's In it For Me?" and "What's in It for You?" in steps 2 and 5 above. Reconsider "Know the Wants and Needs" from Step 7, "Take Aim." Make sure to review the goals you established in the beginning. Meanwhile, continue to focus on the wants and needs of your audience, too.

If your audience adopts your idea, that should help you achieve and accomplish your goals, as well. By helping your audience overcome their conflicts, confrontations, and tensions, you accomplish your personal and organizational goals.

Your idea is a tool, and your audience is the hero.

That's a story worth telling to everybody.

A Question for You

What does success look like for your audience?

_____

_____

_____

_____

_____

What does success look like for you?

_____

_____

_____

_____

_____

Do you feel prepared to communicate your idea?

_____

_____

_____

_____

What other work do you need to do in order to become more prepared?

_____

_____

_____

_____

You have just finished Step 11, "Push the Buttons," in which you told your story and communicated your idea to your audience with some urgency so you could be more compelling and help them overcome their challenge and solve their problem—offering your idea as a tool to help make them a hero. The process doesn't end here. Based on what you learned and picked up on along the process, depending on your audience's reaction and response, you can re-enter the process at any point to improve your preparation and better plan to communicate your idea next time. Take what you've learned, apply it, and continue to improve your communication continually. I wish you all the luck and success throughout this endeavor. If you need my help at all, do not hesitate to reach out to me. We can explore the options available to us.

Conclusion

Thus ends your exploration of the 11 steps to selling innovation that I've identified, field tested, and refined during my decades of work as a journalist, community organizer, marketer, and educator. As I mentioned, this isn't entirely a linear process, even though I've done my best to present it as such. That's what happens while you're communicating: Your audience's response and reaction to your idea can return you to Step 7, "Take Aim," or Step 8, "Be Prepared," during which you refine and improve your communications plan.

Communicating with your audience can even return you to Step 2, "Land on an Ask," at which point you might adjust, improve, and refine your ask and offer. You might even find that you're able to make improvements and refinements at other steps along the way, too.

Consider this 11-step process and experience as an opportunity to continually learn, and to improve and adjust your idea and offer specifically for your target audience. You might fall short the first time. I know that at various stages of my career, I've had to pitch an idea to multiple people at multiple times—in different ways—before something stuck enough to proceed.

One of those ideas—that I move from New York City to Los Angeles in order to be closer to my son, when no one else on my team was based there—literally changed my life. I had to pitch that idea at least three times, to three different people. It might have been four. Regardless, the stakeholder, the need, the value, the time, and the place didn't quite align until that final time. And my life is all the better for it.

Pay attention, accept any failures and shortcomings, and make changes with an eye and mind toward continuous improvement. Never stop trying. Feedback is a gift, and failure is an event, not a characteristic or aspect of your personality or professional capability.

And if you think I can help you at all, with writing and editing services, document review, coaching and mentoring, consulting, a training program or workshop for your team or department, or a talk at a conference or convention, let me know.

I can't wait to hear more about your idea—and help you learn how to communicate it better.

Acknowledgements

I would first like to thank my mother, sister, and father for surrounding me with love and support, and sharing a love of reading and writing over the years. I grew up in a home full of books, magazines, newspapers, comic books, and learning. Working as a magazine editor, and English teacher and community organizer, my parents showed me the value of communication and education early on. I love corresponding with you via letters and emails—especially enjoying my sister's text messages—and look forward to future book exchanges.

I would like to thank my wife, Caitlin Dixon, for sharing a life and home full of experiences, learning, self-development, reading, and writing. Thank you for your patience with my many books, magazines, newspapers, and comic books; and thank you for recognizing and understanding the value of new ideas and insights. As a writer, editor, reader, and storyteller yourself, you continue to delight and inspire me. I will love you forever.

Thank you to my son, Jonah, as well. You are growing up to be an inspiring young man, and I am proud to be your dad. I also have a lot of fun with you. May your love of books, games, learning, and music stay strong for the rest of your life. May your leadership and communication skills continue to develop and improve. Always keep an open mind. Seek new experiences. Never stop learning.

I appreciate and value everything that I learned from Alan Weber and Bill Taylor, founding editors of *Fast Company* magazine. As the 17th employee of arguably the fastest-growing magazine in the history of publishing, I learned more about leadership and innovation, journalism and storytelling, and work and business from you than from anyone else in my career. I also got to meet some of the most creative, interesting, and productive people in the world through the Company of Friends, our pre-social media readers network. Thank you for giving me the opportunity to build something wonderful, and to help other people tell each other their stories.

I am extremely grateful to Dana Atchley, space cowboy and digital storytelling pioneer. My time with you was brief, but I miss you every day. Thank you for sharing your ideas and insights on using new media and technology to tell meaningful stories. You helped me find and share my own story at an important, formative time. Thank you also to Denise Atchley for supporting Dana's work and legacy, and to Joe Lambert and Nina Mullen for their work through the Center for Digital Storytelling, now StoryCenter.

I deeply appreciate the experience and wisdom of Dan Hanson, former Vice President at Land O' Lakes and author of the book *Cultivating Common Ground: Releasing the Power of Relationships at Work.* Your support and advice was invaluable and helped me launch my career as a professional speaker.

Thank you to the event organizers in Belgium, Canada, Denmark, England, Finland, Germany, Holland, Ireland, Italy, Mexico, Norway, Sweden, Switzerland, Ukraine, and the United States who invited me to speak at their conferences or lead workshops at their events. Special thanks are due to Hugh Forrest, Chief Programming Officer for South by Southwest, for including me in the early years of SXSW Interactive. Stay weird, sir.

I would like to thank Chris Brogan, Kevin Eikenberry, Steve Farber, Keith Ferrazzi, Mark Goulston, Jackie Huba and Ben McConnell, Bill Jensen, David Meerman Scott, Dan Pink, Tim Sanders, Stephen Shapiro, Tom Vanderbilt, and Peter Winick for thinking my work was interesting and important enough to highlight in your books, *The New York Times*, and other writing—or otherwise encourage and support. I continue to follow your work attentively and draw energy from your ideas and involvement. Thank you, Dr. Joe Vitale, for your mentoring, constructive criticism, and kind words. And special thanks to Tim Sanders for contributing the Foreword to this volume, my first book as the sole author. You are a role model and inspiration to me. I would also like to thank Seth Godin, founder and CEO of Do You Zoom. In the one year I worked with you as senior director of community development for Squidoo, you taught me a lot about making the professional personal and the personal professional. Thank you especially for the Zig Ziglar CDs. Inviting me to be part of the Group of 33 and co-author *The Big Moo: Stop Trying to Be Perfect and Start Being Remarkable* was an opportunity I didn't take advantage of fully at the time. But I remember one piece of advice in particular: showing up is 80 percent of life. I continue to be inspired by your personal and professional approach to work, your productivity, and your unfettered delight in new ideas.

I would like to acknowledge Rick Bruner, CEO of Central Control. Thank you for the introduction—and entry point—to the profession of marketing research and insights development. My time with you at Doubleclick—continuing to this day on the Research Wonks mailing list—helped me start the second act of my career and continue building on a foundation of communication and learning about people, products, companies, attitudes, interests, and other topics that matter.

I would also like to acknowledge Howard Greenstein, Karen North, Clint Schaff, and the faculties, staffs, and students of New York University and University of Southern California in Los Angeles for welcoming me into the classroom to teach extension and master's degree courses in online journalism and marketing research. I remain in contact with several students and am inspired by the directions their continuing education, careers, and work have taken them.

Thank you to my boss, Priti Mehra, Kevin Taylor, and the other members of Google's Insights Lab, Brand Studio, Marketing, User Experience Research, and Learning and Development teams. Every day I come to work with some of the smartest people, most important ideas, and newest technologies. I appreciate your focus on helpfulness, the people using our products and services, and our collective desire to organize the world's information and make it universally accessible and useful.

Specific to this book project, I'd like to express my gratitude and appreciation to my publisher, *New York Times* bestselling author Raymond Aaron, and my book coach Naval Kumar for believing in the project and helping me commit to putting these ideas—and my work experience—down on paper. Thank you for believing that these ideas were important enough to communicate. Thank you, as well, to my able book cover designer, Waqas Ahmed, and hella skilled interior designer, Mark Lerner of Rag and Bone Shop. I've worked with Mark on multiple projects and will do so again in the future. I owe a brief expression of gratitude to Joshua Sprague, whose 30-Day Book Writing Challenge and friendly email support provided helpful encouragement at key points of my writing process. Very late in the writing process, I reconnected with Michael Margolis, whose deep read, energetic friendship, and generous feedback I utilized fully during my final revisions. I'd also like to recognize the brave early readers who bought the book before I was even done writing it: Brigette Kidd, Jeremy Pepper, Clint Schaff, Stephen Shapiro, Kurt Squire, Jon D. Swartz, and Dan Yrigoyen. Thank you for not asking me to refund your money—even though I offered. You received the book before anyone else!

I value and respect Mykel Board, Tom Burg, Ken Gordon, Kristin Gorski, Chris Heuer, Noel Hidalgo, Souris Hong, Jeremy Pepper, Steve Portigal, Stevyn Prothero, Steve Provizer, Kurt Squire, Levi Stahl, Josh Weinberger, Phil Wolff, and my many other friends, "followers," and people I follow on Twitter (http://twitter.com/h3athrow). Thank you for helping make social media worth participating in—and for sharing your experiences, ideas, and recommendations in 280 characters or less.

Last but not least, a hearty thank you to the subscribers and readers of my weekly email newsletter, *Media Diet* (https://linktr.ee/h3athrow). You are 123 of the smartest and most widely read people I know. I'll see you in your inbox next week!

Since 2008, Heath Row has worked as a researcher for Google Inc., most recently as the Research Operations Manager for Google's Insights Lab, an internal think-and-do tank. As such, he oversees research operations, manages supplier relations, and leads global learning and development programs. Previously, he served as Editorial and Community Director for *Fast Company* magazine for almost a decade. There, he founded the Company of Friends, a pre-social media readers network in which *Fast Company* readers, business leaders, and innovators met online and offline to develop skills, solve problems, and communicate about ideas. He also helped launch and edited *Fast Company*'s Web site.

Heath has also taught undergraduate- and graduate-level classes at New York University and the University of Southern California's Annenberg School for Communication and Journalism. He is a graduate of Northwestern University's Medill School of Journalism. And Heath enjoys comic books, monster movies, backpacking, camping, and hiking.

Heath offers a wide range of personal and professional development programs, resources, and tools. If you'd like to consider and explore working with him in terms of coaching, consulting, professional speaking engagements, training, workshops, or other leadership-, marketing-, and innovation-related capacities, contact him via https:// linktr.ee/h3athrow.

He'll be happy to communicate about ideas with you!

Made in the USA
Middletown, DE
18 May 2021